the
SPIRITUAL
JOURNEY

The Part No One Talks About

ALLYSON ROBERTS

The Spiritual Journey
The Part No One Talks About

Allyson Roberts

ISBN: 978-1-7375511-2-6 (paperback)
ISBN: 978-1-7375511-3-3 (eBook)

Library of Congress Control Number: 2022906327

Printed in Woodstock, Georgia, USA by Allyson Roberts.

The author and publisher have used their best efforts and have strived to be as accurate and complete as possible in the creation of this book.

The advice and strategies found within may not be suitable for every situation. This work is sold with the understanding that neither the author nor the publisher is held responsible for the results accrued from the advice in this book.

While all attempts have been made to verify information provided for this publication, the publisher assumes no responsibility for errors, omissions, or contrary interpretation of the subject matter herein.

For more information, visit AllysonRoberts.com.

TABLE OF CONTENTS

A Special Gift from Allyson

Now that you have your copy of *The Spiritual Journey: The Part No One Talks About*, you are on your way to understanding that even when the world seems to be falling apart, you are a powerful manifestor! Plus … I hope my story helps you understand how much you are loved by the Universe and that perfection is not expected of you in order to build the life you want to live.

You'll also receive the special bonus I created to add to your toolkit … **The Reset**, which is a guided meditation for you to connect with your angels, guides, and masters so that you can wipe your emotional slate clean and continue your journey feeling renewed.

There's so much confusing information out there about spirituality and manifesting. When you finish this book you'll be armed with what you need to know about creating the life your heart desires without having to do it perfectly or be perfect.

While this meditation is offered for sale, just go to the link below and tell us where to send it.

https://www.allysonroberts.com/resetmeditation

The sooner you know how to begin visualizing and attracting everything you want into your life, the better your chances of no longer attracting things you *don't want!*

I'm in your corner. Let me know if I can help further.

Here's to manifesting your best life!

Best,

Allyson

DEDICATION

I'd like to thank my Grandmother Harris for always believing in me, even when she didn't understand me, and my dad, Ned Harris, for loving me unconditionally and supporting me even when I refused to accept his love and help. I'd also like to thank Neal and Marcia Machek for loving my son as their own, and for allowing me the opportunity to participate fully in his wedding when they absolutely didn't have to open their arms to me on his special day.

I'd also like to thank my first therapist, Sally, for believing in me completely. You changed my life. May you rest in the eternal peace that you deserve.

ACKNOWLEDGEMENTS

I'd like to start by acknowledging someone I've yet to give my love and attention to and that is you, the person reading this. Without you, my story wouldn't have nearly the meaning it holds in my heart each time I share it. Without you, my reason to write would be lost. So, thank you for being with me all these years. It makes all the difference.

I'd further like to thank Laura Lindsey for carefully editing each word to make sure that my message reaches you the way it's intended. Her countless hours and devotion to the project are everything.

I'd also like to thank Diana Needham, my publishing and launch strategist, for overseeing this complex project and being the glue that held it all together from start to finish.

And last but certainly not least, a special shoutout goes to Carri Betts and Amor Fernandez for being the first eyes on this story and sharing their honest feedback.

INTRODUCTION
THE QUESTIONS WE ASK OURSELVES

Have you ever been in the middle of something that feels sort of crazy and asked yourself, "How in the hell did I end up here, again?" It's actually a pretty common question, especially when you think the healing process is over only to find yourself struggling again. It can be so frustrating.

Have you ever been in a situation and prayed, hoped, or wished that the circumstances would change so everything could finally get better? I remember complaining about my family to my very first therapist (I was nineteen), and her question to me was, "Why do they have to change for you to be peaceful? Why not change your patterns and then let the chips fall where they may?"

I recall thinking she was insane. Then, after I thought about it for a minute, I realized she was onto something. After all, at that point, I'd waited nineteen years for something to give, to no avail.

After a couple of years in therapy, I decided it would be a great idea to convert to Catholicism. My therapist was Jewish so it had nothing to do with her. It was more that after going through a crisis, not to mention years of childhood abuse, I felt I'd finally found some normalcy in my life. What I didn't realize is the path I was taking was a dangerous one. Not because I was becoming Catholic, but more because I was replacing my attention on myself with an obsession with the church.

Attending daily Mass was my ritual to numb everything. I didn't miss a day. At 7 a.m. every morning, there I was, on my knees praying and standing in line to receive a blessing. I wasn't yet worthy enough for communion. That wouldn't come for another six months after a grueling schedule of classes, Mass, and community service. While I understand that religion certainly has its place for some, it wasn't healthy for me. It was, for me, a fortress shielding me from internal tortures that I truly believed would go away so long as I attended church and acted as best I could.

Have you ever felt this way? Have you ever been sitting in any kind of worship service or meditation wondering how in the hell your life could be so bad when you were behaving so well? It's a question I found myself asking quite frequently. It seemed the more I tried to fix my life with "being the good girl," the messier it turned out to be.

The reason? I wasn't being my true authentic self. I was wearing an entire wardrobe of masks – one to match every occasion – and I was slowly slipping into a delusion that religion solved everything. "Just pray." I must have heard that hundreds of times. While I love God and accept Jesus has been incredibly influential in my life, this life wasn't working for me. My problems were getting larger than life.

If you can relate to any of this, then you've landed in a good place. Here is where you will (finally) feel seen and heard. It's a place of comfort and belonging.

Allow me to introduce myself. My name is Allyson Roberts. I am an experienced life coach with a Cognitive Behavioral background. I'm also a trauma expert, having lived with it twenty-four hours a day, seven days a week growing up – and then becoming certified in understanding and healing it. I'm a bestselling author, and an international speaker, and will be giving my first Blu Talk this year. If you aren't familiar with it, think Ted Talk, except it's spiritually based. I'm incredibly excited to be joining Corey Poirier on stage!

Enough about me. This is your time to grab a pen, whatever beverage you prefer, perhaps a snack to go with it, and join me as you follow along on some of the most complex and difficult times of my life. It's not just about me, though. At the end of each chapter, you'll have the opportunity to explore right alongside me. You can use that time to reflect, look deeper within, and make some serious decisions about the next steps on your path without spiritually bypassing any part of your pain.

Let's get started.

CHAPTER ONE

SEDONA

We were all seated around a large table in a small room. It was the end of the day, and after teaching for twelve straight hours, I was worn out. Relieved that someone else would be handling our evening session, I settled in.

Mark would be leading us in the tea leaf reading, and I was thrilled to find out what was in store for me. I only had one such reading before, and the woman who read for me shared that I was heading for success. It was a low time in my life, and hearing that carried me through some tough months as I lost everything in the 2008 real estate crash. Even though my life is now pretty amazing, I still wanted to know what great things Mark would find inside my cup.

How it works, if you aren't familiar with tea leaf readings, is that you are given a mug with loose tea leaves, and the facilitator pours hot water over them. After the tea steeps for several minutes, each person drinks the tea carefully so as not to swallow the leaves. After the water is gone, the leaves left behind tell a story of what is happening in that person's life.

While the tea was steeping, Mark guided us through a meditation. We were instructed to picture white fluffy clouds resting against a crystal blue sky. As the clouds formed in my mind, I saw strong animals, including a gorilla, bear, jaguar, and snake. It was beautiful watching each form, and I felt strongly that they were coming to remind me of my inner strength.

Next, I saw a plane skywriting. The first message covered the sky – "You are safe." I breathed in deeply. Something stirred inside me as emotions were ignited. As the leader and teacher of a six-day retreat, I had been feeling everyone's energy from love to fear. Navigating through their journeys alongside them, it had become challenging to protect my energy. I had also been sick the second day after being fed gluten at a local restaurant. I'm allergic to it, so I endured three hours of vomiting to the point of utter exhaustion, and my skin was bruised from how hard I was scratching. To make matters even more stressful, my daughter called the day before with the news that she had tested positive for COVID. I felt helpless being so far from home.

Mark's voice brought me back to the meditation, and I felt grateful for every person in the room with me. I reconnected to the fluffy clouds and blue sky. We were guided to continue seeing shapes in the cloud formations. Suddenly, the clouds were gone, and the airplane was back. It began skywriting and, to my horror, it wrote, "I'm insignificant." The plane disappeared as I sat in my chair shaking.

As the leader of this group, I was fighting the emotions rising inside me.

No, no, no, Allyson. I started to panic. *Keep your shit together.*

Thinking that maybe I didn't understand the exact context of the word, I took a break from the meditation and quickly looked it up on my phone. The words stared back at me: Too small or unimportant to be worth consideration. There it was. For fifty-six years, I hadn't been able to explain how my upbringing and trauma had deeply impacted me on a subconscious level. I was raised by a narcissistic mother who consistently made me and my siblings feel insignificant. She had been successful in planting that idea deep into my mind. I had a realization in the meditation though; labeling her as a narcissist only describes her condition, but I had never been able to express how her mental illness makes me feel and how it has impacted my life.

As everyone in the room was coming out of their meditation, I found myself furiously wiping tears from my face. I couldn't wipe them away fast enough. I would wipe one, and ten would fall. I would wipe those ten, and dozens more poured out. I was losing this emotional battle.

There was a side door that opened to a patio with chairs. It was adjacent to the fitness center and outdoor pool area. I escaped through that door and fell into a chair. My five-year-old Allyson was falling apart, and I wasn't stopping her. She needed to release this deep anguish. My adult self also released what felt like a million attacks on my heart.

Carri, my assistant coach, rushed outside and held me while allowing me to empty it all. People were walking by, and I didn't care. I'm sure my wailing unnerved them. I didn't care about that, either. I have always made sure everyone else was okay around me, held my shit together, and carried on. Not this time.

After several minutes, I pulled myself together as Carri and I took deep breaths. She asked me if I was ready to go back into the meditation room. I thought I was, so we rejoined the group. However, as soon as I sat down, someone asked if I was okay, and I couldn't contain the pain. I started weeping uncontrollably. All of my clients witnessed a complete breakdown from their leader – their anchor. For a split second, I was humiliated, but then the vision of the first message of skywriting came back to me, "You are safe." I trusted it and poured my heart out into a puddle of tears. As I tried to explain what was going on, everyone came to my verbal rescue.

"That's just your reptilian brain!"

"We love you. Stop!"

"You're not insignificant."

The words were being thrown simultaneously, and while I felt all the love, I knew I had to use this as a teaching moment. I explained that it was the first time in my life I was accepting that my mother is incapable of love and how sad I feel for her and all of us in her family. I also shared that it's okay to not be okay.

Sometimes we need to feel awful. We need to allow our pain to surface. Otherwise, it will show up in areas of our lives that we least expect. Our relationships, our health, and our finances can be impacted by unprocessed pain. Most of us want to "fix" the external issues because they are easier to identify, and because we can usually find tangible solutions. Very few people, however, are unwilling to repair what's going on internally. It is so easy to hide behind false personas like happy pictures on social media and big paychecks. Many coaches try to "fix" other people to feel better about themselves, yet they never do their deep work to take their practice one step further. That's not me, and that's not how I want to coach myself or others.

Vulnerability is scary as hell for me, yet, my guides reminded me before my "insignificant breakdown" (and breakthrough) that I'm safe. After the shock of it all, I paced my hotel room, asking some deep questions of myself and my guides.

Why did I have to break down in front of other people?

The answer was so simple and beautiful. "Allyson, they love you, and they needed to see that you are human, and you felt supported."

At that moment, I realized the first message started with "You," while the second began with "I'm." It was as if my angels and guides wrote the first message for me, and my inner child Allyson wrote the second. She needed to show me how she's been feeling her entire life. She knew I would be supported. She sensed that we would be okay and that I would be able to process that deep pain among people who accept me.

Peace flooded my heart and soul. I piled pillows in front of the fireplace and stared into the dancing flames. My mother taught me how to love deeply and completely despite her hatred, slaps, scratches, punches, evil words, and selfish deeds. Through all of her abuse, I still learned how to honor myself. As insufferable as she made our existence, I managed to learn compassion, empathy, and love. As I sat watching the fire, feeling the warmth on my face, I couldn't help but notice how cold the rest of the room was. It reminded me of my childhood. It was mainly cold, but warmth would flood in from unexpected places every once in a while. As much as he struggled with expressing emotion, my dad also gave me enough love over the years to keep me grounded.

At last, I suddenly knew that I didn't have to settle anymore. At that moment, I felt my worth and how important my work is to the world. For a split second, my mother's voice flooded in.

Who do you think you are? You're not important. You'll never amount to anything. You're so lazy! Spread your legs. Maybe that will get you somewhere. My mother's shrill, unnerving voice, though only in my mind, pierced through my core.

The times I'd done my best to stand up to her, she would get this eerie calm about her, look me straight in the eyes, and tell me I was crazy. After hearing it enough times, you start to believe the gaslighting.

I shook her voice out of my head and brought myself back to my hotel room; I was back beside the cozy fireplace. Just then, something happened that I was merely an observer to. I sat and watched her standing at my bedroom door shrieking while that venom flowed out of her. I could see her face clearly and finally saw her fragmented soul with my eyes closed. My heart hurt, but I was also free to understand that those words were meant for herself. They never had anything to do with me. I stood and walked into the bathroom to prepare for much-needed sleep. As I looked in the mirror, I saw my exhausted but peaceful reflection gazing back at me.

Allyson, you're not crazy; you're powerful.

I kept eye contact with myself for a few moments and accepted that maybe everything would be okay after all. Maybe, just maybe, I'm worthy enough to have everything my heart desires. Perhaps I'm not crazy, but a loving healer who understands how the brain works more than most people. Maybe I'm the pain master, meaning that I get the power of healing, and I'm a master at helping others heal.

For a second, I felt a pang of shame. How dare I think such amazing things about myself? Who am I to believe this about myself? As I looked back at my reflection, I saw myself for the first time instead of seeing my mother's child. Finally…freedom.

Intuition

Do you trust your intuition?

_____

_____

_____

When was the last time you felt your intuition nudging you?

_____

_____

_____

_____

Do you feel like your true and authentic self?

_____

_____

_____

If you could make a wish for your life, what would you wish for?

_____

_____

_____

_____

Being able to visualize what you want is one of the first steps to getting back in touch with the core of you. Congratulations for being here and for being honest. You can't heal what you refuse to acknowledge.

CHAPTER TWO

SWEET TEA

I was standing in the cold, smoking one of who knows how many cigarettes of the day. I was three packs down and needed more. In my server's apron was a piece of cardboard leftover from the over one hundred orders I had taken in an almost non-stop shift between Friday night, Saturday and Sunday. A Calculus exam would be waiting for me the following day. College was proving quite the challenge for this homeless, directionless girl. I was eighteen. Completely alone. Lost. Confused. Angry. And cold. Everything felt frozen.

My manager, Alan, walked outside and stood next to me. I don't think we said anything to one another for a solid five minutes. He didn't smoke, so he was just standing there. Thinking back, I can't even imagine how I must have reeked with the odors of grease from the kitchen, trash from many trips to the dumpster that night, and the wretched smell leftover from a nicotine habit that was my only vice.

"Allyson, there's just really no other way to say this." Alan never used more words than he had to. I braced myself for the worst. "You need therapy," Alan spoke deliberately while looking directly at me. I tried to avoid making eye contact by any means necessary.

I surprised myself with how still and quiet I remained as I allowed his words to land in unfamiliar places. I knew he was right because Alan was always right. He had the calmest demeanor of anyone I had ever met. The day I walked into his family-owned restaurant, I had been living on a friend's couch for nine months. I was homeless, exhausted, broke, desperate, and eager to learn.

"Have you ever served tables before?" Alan asked me as I nervously stood near a booth that needed cleaning.

"No, sir." I felt defeated, but with determination in my voice, I explained, "But my first job was at a shoe store in the mall, and I had to take off customers' shoes and socks before helping them into new shoes. I can handle myself really well."

"Well, you'll be relieved here, then," Alan spoke through laughter. "It's just food. You're hired."

He loved my work ethic because I picked up every available shift, covered for anyone who needed time off, and many days after work I would take the bus to the battered women's shelter where I interned. After long nights at the shelter, I would take the train to school. I owned a little Volkswagen Beetle, but I never had enough money to put gas in it between books, meals, rent, cigarettes, and toiletries. My life was hustle and grind. There wasn't time to think about everything I had been through growing up, and I had no real plan for the future. I lived day-to-day in survival mode.

When Alan told me I needed therapy, I knew he was right, but no part of me wanted to go. No one in my family had ever been to therapy, and the only experience I had with any psychologist was when I was four or five years old. Someone called the Department of Children Services on my mother, and I was made to visit their child psychologist along with my older brother. My mother drove us to the facility, and the trip felt like an eternity.

"If you say anything about what's going on at home, you will never see each other again or your two sisters!" My mother scowled at us through the rearview mirror.

The thought of never seeing my favorite sister, who was practically raising me, was enough to keep my lips tightly sealed. This group of men came to collect me from the waiting room and took me into this small, dark room. They placed a picture in front of me and wanted me to tell a story. The image was of a dragon inside a cave. I froze. No words could even find their way to my mouth. After quite a long time of sitting in silence, their voices raised in frustration. One of the men slammed his fist on the table and grimaced at me.

"What do you see, Allyson?" He looked so disappointed in me. I felt shame pulsing through my veins.

What he didn't understand was how much violence I was experiencing at home. I learned to freeze when voices were raised because it almost always led to punches being thrown. There was no getting me to speak after his outburst. I felt unsafe, and there was no coming back. I was unable to tell any sort of story about the dragon in the cave.

Back inside the car, my mother was victorious. She pulled a cigarette from her purse, rolled down the windows, and chain-smoked back to our prison cell of a home. I was defeated. My brother was defeated. She knew it and was never happier.

"Let's go inside," Alan's voice brought me back to the diner parking lot. He opened the door for me, motioning inside, "It's freezing out here." Once inside, he coaxed me to a booth and gently asked, "Coffee or Coke?" I pointed to the coffeemaker. My hands were numb, and I needed to warm up.

"Here you go." Alan handed me a huge white mug filled with the hot, comforting coffee. His kindness left its mark on me as I slowly sipped and tried to give him my attention.

"Listen," Alan picked our conversation back up. "You're an amazing person. You are. But something is going on with you, and I'm just telling you as a friend, you need therapy. I know a woman. She's young, but she's great." I stared out the café window. Suddenly, snow started to come down.

"Oh no! I gotta go! The buses will shut down soon. I can't…." I stood to leave.

Alan stood up with me and held up his hand in front of me. Then he said something that caused my direction in life to pivot in a way I wasn't expecting.

"Allyson, if you don't get therapy, I'm going to have to let you go. I can't watch you smoke yourself to death. I can't watch you scream at the garbage bags anymore, cuss at the coffee pot, and kick the walls when you think no one is looking. You're angry. You're great with the customers, and I love that, but your personal life is in the shitter." He continued as I fell back into my seat, "You have so much potential! You do. You have an amazing heart, but if you can't do this for yourself, at least do it for your paycheck." His eyes held true concern for me, something that I hadn't felt from anyone for longer than I wanted to admit. I was angry and in denial, but deep down I knew he was right.

Three weeks flew by, and I had already participated in four counseling sessions. One of the first steps my therapist convinced me to take was to stop taking the bus when I had a perfectly good car. She told me I needed to be disciplined enough to put eight dollars into my gas tank every two weeks. This also meant paying for parking at the garage at school, which was three dollars a day. It was a substantial financial commitment for me, and it was stressing me out. Looking back, I realize it wasn't about the money at all but the freedom that having my vehicle gave me. Freedom wasn't something I was at all comfortable with, and even though I was away from the narcissistic monster that raised me, emotionally and mentally I found myself still functioning as if she was lurking around every corner. My mother's abuse had traumatized me to the point that I didn't know how to live, only how to survive.

Alan wasn't kidding about the therapist being young. Alice was in her mid-twenties if I had to guess. She was highly awkward in her approach with me, but she was brutally honest, which I desperately needed. I would later learn that Alice was Alan's niece, and he talked to her about me many times. She was the one who convinced him to strongarm me into counseling. Alan knew I didn't want to lose my job, but more than anything, I didn't want to lose the stable feeling Alan gave me at work and I think he knew that too. He was the only man who didn't seem to want sex from me. Alan never hinted at it, and while he was happily married, that had never really mattered to most men that came into my life. They all seemed to eventually want me in their bed. It would always leave me feeling disgusting and unworthy of true success. Alan never made me feel unsafe or unheard, which made me deeply appreciate the connection we had.

In therapy, unlike at work and school, I couldn't hide. After a while, though, I didn't want to hide anymore. I found myself telling Alice stories about my childhood that I could never share with anyone. There was one particular day where Alice had me focusing on shedding shame and guilt over things I had no control over. With her invitation to release that pain, I found a truth that I had always known and suppressed.

"I wanted to choose my dad in the divorce," I cried to Alice, holding onto a pillow I had become all too familiar with. "She stopped me. She threatened me. I was only ten years old!" I wailed into the pillow so hard I felt my body could snap in half at any moment. I was finally being vulnerable, and it hurt in all of the best ways.

Alice, per usual, sat in poised silence as I processed what I was saying. The words felt too real. I was back in that car with my mom on the way to the courthouse. I could hear her voice in my ear so clearly.

"Your father doesn't even love you," she sneered, "He doesn't care if you eat or have anything you need. He doesn't even want to pay child support. And you know even if you do go with him, he's never going to want to be home with *you!* He was never home when it was all of us in one house, you think he's going to change *just for you?*" Her cackling, mimicking laughter echoed in my mind and I could smell her perfume. It was making me feel nauseated.

Alice gave me time to compose myself, and when she felt I was ready to continue she asked calmly, "What happened when you had the chance to testify?"

"My mom's attorney asked me who I wanted to live with and I just…" Taking a deep breath, I looked down at the tear-soaked pillow. "I froze. He pushed me and pushed me until I finally answered, no, whispered actually, that I wanted to live with my mom. It was an answer given out of complete fear and exhaustion." I took another deep breath and stared off into the distance.

"I still remember the heartbreak on my dad's face. Victory swept over my mom with a crooked smile as she slowly nodded in approval toward me. After her day in court, my mom continued to manipulate me and my dad. On weekends when I was supposed to see him, she would call and tell him I had made other plans and not to come get me. I would wait for him for hours and hours. She wanted me to believe what she told me in the car that day, that my dad didn't want me." I continued to stare at nothing in particular as I spilled my guts to Alice.

I worked with Alice for exactly six months. In that time, I learned so much about myself. While our sessions broke down some of my walls and gave me a lot of hope, I also found myself starting to bypass my pain spiritually. I know Alice did not intend for that to happen and neither did I. When I told Alice that I had found a church, she thought it was wonderful, and she encouraged me to make friends and get involved. The thing is, all the people in the young adult program had their shit together, or at least it seemed like it compared to where I was in life. None of them were experiencing homelessness, none of them seemed to have vices the way I did with cigarettes, and all the girls were either engaged to their boyfriends or set on finding a husband. They all had a set path, a plan that was in motion. They all seemed so sure of themselves. I wasn't anywhere close to that, and I felt utterly alone, a feeling I was all too familiar with and wanted to get away from. After a few weeks, I attended regular services but avoided the social aspect.

One day I had the inspired idea of taking a drive out into the country. My dad always lived in small country towns with dirt roads and cows. Any time I was actually able to visit him, when my mother was unable to intervene, I would soak up time with him outside surrounded by nature and animals. It was peaceful, and the exact opposite of life with my mom. To this day, any time I get too overwhelmed, I can hop in my car and drive to the country where I can feel almost instant relief at the sight of a horse farm or two. My dad had gifted me the Beetle, and it was fun to drive stick shift on gravel roads. Even though I was in a completely different part of the state from my dad, I could feel him with me on that road. The windows were down, the band Journey was blaring, and then *clunk, clunk, clunk*. The car stopped.

"Shit! Shit!" I grunted, immediately aware of what the problem was. I knew I was out of gas because the gauge was broken, and I forgot to fill up. There was no one around. I let out a deep sigh and pulled a cigarette from my purse, got out of the car, and rested on the hood for a while.

I was down to my last cigarette when a white pick-up truck approached from the hillside. As it got closer I saw a head full of curly black hair shining in the summer sun. It was a guy close to my age, and as he rolled to a stop, he flashed a fantastic smile, "Well, it looks like you might need some help." I laughed, "As a matter of fact, I do!" His six-foot frame eagerly jumped from his truck. "Has this happened before?"

I sheepishly grinned, "My gas gauge is busted. I should've known better than to drive out here all by myself, but it's such a beautiful day, and I just wanted some freedom, you know?" My words surprised me.

He gave me a knowing look. "Actually, I do know," he paused, "Well, we can handle this one of two ways: you can either hop in my truck and let's go grab a can of gas, or you can wait here, and I'll be back in about an hour. What's your pleasure?"

I took a long and hard look at him, and before I could say anything, he put his arms up in a defensive gesture, "Look, I'm not going to hurt you, okay? But if you don't believe me, I can just leave you alone, but it'll be dark soon, and I don't want you here by yourself."

"I need cigarettes anyway," I mumbled as I grabbed my purse. We pulled into a Hardee's instead of a gas station. He gestured toward the menu displaying oversized burgers and fries. Smiling with almost perfect teeth, he asked, "You want anything to drink?" I was frustrated, but his smile seemed so genuine. I smiled back at him, "Yeah, I'll take a sweet tea, thanks." I reached for my last cigarette and sighed in relief when I found my lighter.

"Nope, sorry, sweetheart, not around me." The stranger was still smiling at me but it was more a polite smile to sugar coat something he found repulsive. "I can't stand those things."

Embarrassed, I shoved the cigarette back into the box and sank into my seat a little. I wanted to get this strange encounter over with. We pulled into the gas station, which was right across the street.

"Hey, Billy!" A girl about my age bolted out of the gas station door toward the truck. As she got closer Billy let out a sigh. Her blonde curls bounced around and perfectly framed the gas station logo on her shirt.

"Billy, It's good to see ya. How's your daddy and them?" Her bubbly Southern accent reminded me of my mother. I was instantly put off by her, which was possibly unfair to her, but a trigger is what it is. I noticed her giving me the once over. I jumped out of the truck and went inside to get a gas can. It occurred to me that the curly headed boy and I hadn't even introduced ourselves to one another. I could hear their mumbled conversation from inside where I picked out a five-gallon container.

"I was on my way to my parents' house, and this girl was stranded on the road. You know me, I'm not going to let a damsel in distress suffer if I can help it."

She touched his arm, "You're the best, Billy! And your daddy, too! We just all love ya'll!" There was that trigger again. I could basically see my mother in place of this girl, flirting and covertly judging or manipulating situations.

I took a deep breath as I walked back to the truck. She stopped mid-sentence when she saw me. I handed her a five-dollar bill for the gas can and reached for the pump handle when I was interrupted, "No, ma'am!" Billy took my money from his friend, handed it back to me, then yanked the handle from me, "No lady pays or pumps for her gas." This seemed to put our gas attendant on edge, and she quickly turned and went back inside. Billy continued, "By the way, I'm Billy. I can't believe we rode that whole way and I never even asked your name."

In my entire life, I had never been treated like this by a guy. Alan treated me very well but I was his employee. It felt different. I stood motionless and speechless. Billy just kept filling up the gas can and smiling at me, "Do you have a name?" I caught myself, "Oh gosh, yes, sorry. It's Allyson – two L's and a Y."

Billy cocked his head, "That's different. I bet there's a lot of different things about you."

If he only knew.

It was getting dark as we finally pulled up to my car, and I realized that Billy had done most of the talking. I learned a lot about him, from his farm handling to his father's interest in politics, his hometown, his favorite meal. He talked and I listened. It was strange to me that a man just wanted to talk to me. What bothered me, though, was that he had learned basically nothing about me. He knew I smoked, went to college, had a car with a broken gas gauge, preferred sweet tea over Coke, and had no idea how a lady was supposed to be treated at a gas pump. Regardless, he wanted to see me again. I told him I made most of my calls from a payphone at school, so he gave me his telephone number, told me to leave a message on his machine if he didn't answer, and we parted ways.

I got in my car and watched him drive away from the direction of his parents' house and back into town. I waited for the dust to settle on the road, started my car, and drove to the gas station where we had just been. I was surprised to see Billy sitting in his truck when I pulled in. He walked toward my car smiling, "I was hoping you'd come back here to fill up. Can I take you to dinner?" Little did I know that a BBQ sandwich and another sweet tea with this man would alter the course of my life forever.

Decisions

To date, what's the hardest decision you've made?

_____

_____

_____

Were you scared? Yes ____ No ____ Maybe ____

If you had to go back and make the same decision now, would you? Yes ____ No ____

What's the biggest lesson you learned?

_____

_____

_____

_____

_____

From that lesson, if you had a magic wand, what's the next step you would take on your path to improve your current life? Remember, it's just a magic wand, so dream big.

_____

_____

_____

_____

_____

Make a cup of tea, cozy up in a comfortable chair, and come with me on this next leg of my journey.

CHAPTER THREE

FALSEHOOD

Have you ever heard yourself, or someone you love, say, "The next thing I knew..." and go on to explain how the situation, whatever it was, spun out of control? Well, I've come to understand how trauma can cause someone to feel like they're stuck on an emotional rollercoaster where everything feels in control one minute and in chaos the next. The chaos stops when more emphasis is placed on healing, but when we are in pain and throwing action at our discomfort instead of fixing the real problem, life quickly becomes messy!

I know life becomes messy when we are in pain because I lived that story. Billy became a major factor in my journey. To say our romance was a whirlwind makes it seem so cliché. It felt more like a speeding car with no brakes. Fun for a moment until it's not anymore.

Our first date sharing BBQ sandwiches and getting to know each other better led to a kiss under the stars at the end of the night, which led to Billy inviting me to stay in his guest room for a couple of nights instead of going back to my friend's couch. I accepted and two days after moving my stuff into the guest room, we were in the throws of a passionate and whirlwind romance. Suddenly, there we were. A very typical couple living in a cute farmhouse out in the middle of nowhere. It was complete with chickens, goats, two cows, and a baby piglet who sometimes slept with us. For the first time, I convinced myself that I was loved, safe, and "home." Life felt easy.

Billy left for work every morning in his white pickup truck while I attended classes downtown. The drive was hell, but the payoff was worth it. The honeymoon phase paid off in many ways, one being that Billy had finally convinced me to stop smoking. It was a dealbreaker for him and there was no way I was losing the stability I had been craving for a lifetime. I expected quitting to be harder, but I think I was so determined to make Billy proud that I blocked the cravings almost effortlessly. I also quit my job and therapy. After all, my problems were gone, and this great guy was telling me that he was going to take care of me for the rest of my life. Things were never better.

One day while I was sitting in the library at school, I pulled out my calendar and was marking due dates for assignments when I suddenly froze. "Wait," I heard myself say to no one. "Oh no, no, no, no," I whispered in complete panic. I flipped to the previous page and back again a few times. "Shit!" The librarian shot me a look. I jumped up and quickly headed to the restroom. I checked my clothes hoping for a stain that would relieve me of my utter fear.

No, no, no, no, no. NO! I banged my fist against the stall wall. *This isn't happening! Maybe the stress of the move, all the driving, quitting the cigarettes, and the sudden changes... Did I put too much pressure on my body?* I slowly walked back to my books and fell into the chair. I stared at nothing. *How had I let this happen?*

Gathering my things, all I could think about was how Billy would react if I was actually pregnant. I needed to be absolutely certain I was pregnant before telling Billy and knew where I needed to go. I found myself at the pharmacy and made my way to the feminine hygiene aisle. A lump formed in my throat.

I'm on birth control ... How did this happen? I reached into my bag and checked the packaging. No pills were missed. I took them religiously every morning with my coffee. I had no idea which test to pick, and as I pulled one off the shelf marked "early detection" the lump in my throat dropped into my stomach.

I wanted to test right then, but the test required morning urine. I was stuck waiting. My stomach was tight. Billy sensed something was off, but I convinced him it was the pressure of school. He tried to comfort me by boasting about how I had finally gotten out of living on a couch, working at a diner, going to therapy, and to top it all off, we were madly in love. We joked about how things were crazy and could always be worse, but he was taking my pain personally. That's something I never wanted to put on him. All I could think about was his reaction to this news should the test come back positive.

As Billy slept I stared at the ceiling and watched the clock from the corner of my eye. It was 3 a.m. when I felt the urge to pee. Was that early enough to test? I didn't care, I needed to know. I climbed out of bed as quietly as possible, tip-toed to the bathroom, and pulled the test out from the very back of the vanity cabinet where I had hidden it before Billy got home. I sat on the floor and held the test tightly against my chest. I questioned if I truly wanted to find out then and there, but I knew what I had to do. We talked about getting married soon anyway, and I knew Billy wanted kids. Maybe I could pull off making the marriage happen quicker than previously planned, and I could pull off the whole being pregnant thing as a honeymoon gift. The truth is, though, I'm not a good pretender. It would also feel deceitful, and that was not an option for me. I carefully unwrapped the contents of the box, peed on the stick, and waited.

Two minutes later and there it was—the blue plus sign that changed my life permanently. I was pregnant. I couldn't breathe. I sat still, and then the shaking started. My whole body shook as I slumped to the floor. I had my fair share of moments where I felt like a total screw-up before Billy was in my life, but this sealed the deal for me. Life as I knew it was over, and it had just started. All of my dreams were coming true. Even though I knew that Billy had equal responsibility in this, I just couldn't shake the feeling that it was all my fault.

Billy woke to the usual routine in our home. I was in the kitchen making coffee, packing our lunches, and preparing to head out the door for school. He was already showered and dressed in his usual – a flannel shirt, jeans, and his work boots. I felt like a complete fraud kissing him good morning, making small talk, and sharing our first cup of coffee for the day.

"I love you, Allycat!" Billy poked playfully at my ribs as he kissed my forehead, "Go and have yourself a scholarly day, now." He kissed me on the lips and bounced out the door.

I blared the Go-Go Girls on the drive to school and pretended like everything was fine. I planned on taking one more test the following day just to be sure. Maybe it was a false positive, and maybe, just maybe, this nightmare would be over. I knew better, but denial was the only way I could make it through the day. The following day, I went through the same routine all over again, except this time I waited until 4:30 a.m. to test. It turned out just as I suspected – a blue plus sign. *Great. It was time to tell Billy.*

Sitting next to him, I gently woke him with kisses all over his face. He pulled me close, "Hey there, you. What's going on? You scared? Bad dream?"

He caught my eye. "Well, I guess that all depends on you," I caught myself and instantly felt my heart in my throat. I didn't mean to put that sort of pressure on him.

Billy propped himself on his elbows. He wasn't a morning person, so my timing wasn't the best. I knew this. I heard myself just blurt it out – "I'm pregnant."

There was a long, agonizing pause.

The next thing I knew, I was up in the air, being twirled around like a sack of potatoes. Billy was screaming with excitement, "Oh my god! Oh my god! Are you sure? Are you serious? Oh no! I'm so sorry. Are you okay? I didn't hurt you, did I?" He placed me back down gently.

My heart burst with joy! This man was perfect. I knew it the moment we shared lunch, but now it was confirmed. I assured him I was fine, ran into the bathroom, grabbed the test, and danced back to him.

After all the excitement, we couldn't fall back to sleep, so we went to our usual Waffle House for breakfast before heading our separate ways. We spent the entire meal brainstorming names, talking about the nursery, and how Billy was going to teach his kid everything he knew about construction and property development, and which he said he would proudly do even if our baby was a girl. It was tough leaving each other. We hugged so long in the parking lot that someone drove by and playfully shouted for us to get a room. Billy announced our news to the stranger, who then softened and congratulated us. I was in a dream.

After classes, I couldn't wait to be home. It was Thursday, which meant it was pizza night followed by watching our favorite show, *Dallas*, but when I pulled into our driveway there was a car parked where Billy's truck would usually be. I immediately recognized it – Billy's father. My stomach dropped. As I got closer to the front door I could hear his dad.

"No son of mine is going to marry a whore! It's bad enough that she's shacking up with you, but *a baby*, son! I won't have it! You're also not even thinking about your poor mother. She's going to have a heart attack. Do you know how hard it is for her to put a smile on her face and talk about your wedding? If we allow this, it's going to be a shotgun wedding! Grow up!"

I gathered every ounce of courage I had and opened the door. Billy's face fell. At that moment I didn't care about his conservative, overbearing father. I just wanted to be next to Billy. I made my way to the couch and sat down as close to my fiancé as possible. Billy didn't move, which wasn't like him. He'd typically take my hand, kiss me, but not tonight. I felt glaring eyes of authority on me.

"You will have an abortion if you want to marry my son." The monster pulled a check from his pocket. "I'll even help you out and pay for it. I don't care how much money it will take to erase this mistake. Just get rid of it and do it now."

An evil silence lingered. Billy couldn't take the tension any longer. He stood, slowly walked to the front door, and motioned his father to leave. Before he left, Billy's dad made one last point to stand his ground.

"I mean it, son." His words stabbed me.

Once we were alone, Billy walked halfway up the stairs, asked me to take him to get this truck in the morning, and went to bed. I sat frozen in fear and confusion, wide awake, and before I knew it I was watching the sun come up through our oversized living room window. Feeling numb was all too familiar.

It took a few days to get an appointment at the abortion clinic. During that time, Billy wasn't home much. He had hardly spoken to me since the tongue lashing from his father. Stonewalling in general caused me to panic, but when it was coming from Billy it made the usual panic ten times worse. I was feeling every emotion imaginable except happiness. My happiness was stolen, and at nineteen years old I was being asked to have an abortion to save my relationship.

The day came for the abortion. Billy refused to take me to my appointment. Looking back at his decision, I am torn between accepting that he couldn't follow through with his father's marching orders or he was in deep denial, but for whatever reason, I ended up driving myself. I considered asking friends to take me, but that didn't feel right. When the receptionist asked if I had a ride home, I lied.

Standing at the counter, I was asked more questions about my pregnancy. I gazed around at the lockers against one of the walls, the plain, uncomfortable-looking chairs filled with women looking ashamed and sad, and I caught my own reflection in a two-way window behind some of the chairs. Seeing myself brought immediate shame. I could have sympathy and compassion for the other women around me, but not for myself. Even though I'm pro-choice and I believe women should have the legal right to choose abortion, this felt so wrong in so many ways. We had been so happy just days before, planning out our lives together as parents to this baby inside of me.

After filling out a stack of paperwork, I returned to the window. "It won't be long now," the receptionist reassured me while sounding way too cheerful. I immediately didn't like her. She handed me a key to the same lockers I had been staring at, a hospital gown that felt like sandpaper, and a giant maxi pad. I suppose my face showed confusion because she explained how I would need it following the procedure. A wave of nausea washed over me. *But that's my baby. This is all wrong.*

A nurse took my vitals, another asked me even more intrusive questions about my pregnancy, and before I knew it, there I was, waiting my turn to go behind the two-way mirror. It felt like waiting for the guillotine. Billy's smile flashed in my mind. I pushed it away.

What would dad say about this? Obviously, mother wouldn't give two shits. She would probably laugh at me, scold me, call me names, but still...part of me wonders. Will I be able to get pregnant again? How long is this going to hurt? Does Billy actually want this? I am so lost...

"Allyson," my name echoed down the corridor interrupting my mental spiral.

I slowly stood and followed a woman to a cold, bright room. Two nurses I hadn't seen that morning and a doctor were waiting for me. The doorway seemed to hold me there, and my legs suddenly felt like anchors.

I don't want to do this. I don't want to be here. Why had I agreed to put myself through this hell? None of this makes sense.

One of the nurses sensed my hesitation and approached me with kind eyes. "It's okay. Here, I'll help you." We locked arms as she nudged me toward the bed. Suddenly, orders were being thrown around the room. The doctor was directing the nurses and motioned to me to slide down the bed toward him. The same nurse who helped me into the room was also placing my legs in stirrups on either side of the bed. Everything was moving in slow motion around me except for these three people who seemed to be moving at warp speed. I was shaking like a leaf in the wind, and everyone in the room could sense my tension. One of the nurses suggested that I have something to relax me, and that's when I felt the I.V. going into my arm. A bag was connected at the other end. The nurse told me they would start the medicine as soon as the doctor gave the order.

When I was in high school, life was rough. My world revolved around trying to fit in as best I could to deal with neglect and abuse at home. I had boyfriends who I treated horribly because I couldn't accept kindness. Come to think of it, I wasn't too friendly to the girls, either. That was reciprocated with lies about me and gossip that cut me to my core. Nevertheless, I fought that much harder to find acceptance and approval from everyone.

One of my teachers understood me better than most, taking me under her wing. She gave me extra credit when I failed to turn in assignments. It wasn't that I was lazy; I had zero support at home and I think she could sense it. School supplies, tampons, toilet paper, makeup, new clothes, and shoes were all things purchased by mother for herself and herself only. After she'd leave for work, I would sneak into her room and use things carefully so as not to be missed, but even that proved to be riskier than the reward. During the most challenging times, I started drinking on the weekends with the few people I did socialize with occasionally. I shared this with my teacher, and she told me something that stuck. Her advice was to always think about the next day before doing anything, suggesting that I consider how I feel when I wake up the following day. Her wisdom came flooding back in as I was laying on the cold table with my legs in stirrups.

Before I realized it, I jerked the IV out of my arm, jumped off the table, and ran to my car. I'm sure I could have just told them that I changed my mind. Looking back, it didn't have to be that dramatic, but I was in flight mode. Everything in me was screaming, "RUN!"

My purse and keys were still inside my car. I always left them under the passenger seat. I also had a change of clothes in a duffle bag; I could just leave and act like I was never even there. I left my shoes and other clothes in the locker, and the key was still pinned to my hospital gown. I'm sure I looked like a psych ward escapee. I didn't care.

I placed my head on the steering wheel and sobbed. For the first time in my life, it felt like I finally made a decision solely based on what I wanted, and without concern for how others would feel, but I was absolutely terrified. While it was confirmed that I loved and cared about Billy, I couldn't care less at that moment if he agreed or disagreed with me. All I knew was that our child was conceived in love, and I couldn't end its life.

After gathering myself for a moment, I sheepishly returned to the clinic's reception area. The nurse who had helped me in the operating room greeted me at the door. Without saying a word, she handed back my clothes. As I started to walk back toward my car, she grabbed my arm. "Come change." It wasn't a request but more like an order. In the bathroom, I refused to look at myself. A younger girl was washing her hands as I stepped into a stall to change.

"You're lucky," she half-whispered, "at least you get to decide what you want."

When I finally finished putting on my clothes, I opened the stall door to find the rest of the large wash area empty. I checked each stall to see if she was still there, but she was gone. The bathroom was situated so that when I walked out I couldn't see the waiting area. The same nurse greeted me, gave me a long hug, and told me everything would be okay. I wasn't sure if I believed her, but I knew it was better than the alternative.

Driving home, I thought about that girl's words. I guess, in a way, she was right. I didn't have my narcissistic mother manipulating and controlling me to have an abortion. I could see right through Billy's father and everything he stood for. Billy's mother was a non-issue because she just did whatever her husband ordered her to do. I was also lucky to run out of gas on a dirt road and have Billy find me. I considered myself lucky that he didn't care about my dysfunctional family. I was also lucky that I was in therapy. I felt fortunate that I had quit smoking before getting pregnant. The list of blessings felt great, and my spirits were lifted enough to momentarily quash my fears.

Then I did something that felt awful down to my core – I lied. I told Billy I went through with the abortion. The shame was insurmountable. The fear was even more so. I was caught in a trap I couldn't escape. My maternal instinct took over, though, and I was willing to do anything, sacrifice everything, to keep any harm from coming to my child. My fairytale was over. It didn't even matter. I didn't know what I would do next, but I knew what I wasn't going to do. I've learned that this is the first step at every crossroads. Deciding to reject the wrong direction is the first step to taking us in the right direction. I felt this to be true in the core of my being.

There was also something deeper happening within me. My spiritual connection, or rather a reconnection, was igniting. The feeling and experience were long lost on me. I had given up my hope in religion and Jesus. While I deeply loved Jesus, he seemed more like a cartoon character in the years before Billy. Every prayer to him seemed unanswered, which only left me feeling more alone and abandoned. For me to be talking to Jesus again and reaching out to God while I fed the farm animals and drove to campus was just as much a shock to me as I'm sure it was to the heavens. It felt right, though. I also noticed my intuition turning back on full power, and the restored confidence felt foreign but welcomed. I felt lighter even with all the heaviness around me. Even so, I wanted a sign, so I asked God to let me know, without any doubt, that lying to Billy, for now, was forgivable.

Billy and I went to church with his parents every Sunday. It wasn't a request as much as an order. The family image was everything to Billy's father, and his poor mother just went along with the charade. I felt sorry for her. Billy was just like his mom – sweet, caring, empathetic, and emotionally negligent when it came to anything his father said or did. So, there I was with all nine of Billy's family members taking up an entire pew in the front row. We were dressed to perfection, but underneath it was a mess of adultery, an emotionally abused wife, submissive and settling children, and the newly pregnant liar.

The church minister was irritating. He worked himself up into a yell that I'm sure could be heard throughout the town if anyone cared enough to listen. His sermon that particular day, though, hit me straight between the eyes. He spoke of how Pharaoh demanded that all the Hebrew midwives kill all newborn male babies. Exodus 1:17-21.

"The midwives lied to protect the babies by telling Pharaoh that the women delivered the babies before the midwives could arrive. He believed them, and God rewarded the midwives for their falsehood." It felt like he was speaking directly to me.

Even though I was only eight weeks pregnant, I knew right then and there that I was carrying a boy. I also knew that God would reward me for saving a life. The very next day, however, my faith would be rocked and my world would turn entirely upside down.

Panic

Have you ever panicked?

What caused you to panic?

Do you regret your decision from that place of panic?

If you could go back, what would you do differently?

Did you know that the number one cause of anxiety is regret? Did you also know that ruminating over the past and trying to rewrite what happened can prohibit you from healing the wound the incident caused? In other words, you are bypassing the cure by focusing on the poison.

It's not your fault. Now you know, though. So, what are you willing to do differently so that you can heal?

CHAPTER FOUR

FREEZING COLD

It was freezing out. I woke up at 3 a.m. to a cold house. Billy wasn't in bed. I went downstairs to find him asleep in front of the fireplace that was no longer giving off any warmth. I adjusted the heat, covered him with another blanket, and went upstairs to shower. Final exams were early that day, and I had a lot of last-minute studying to do before heading downtown. With Christmas right around the corner, I was planning on telling Billy the truth on Christmas Eve. I couldn't think of a better time to come clean with him, but God had different plans.

After cleaning up I sat down at our desk upstairs when a wave of nausea like I had never experienced in my life hit me like a tsunami. I barely made it to the bathroom in time before I fell onto the floor violently shaking and vomiting. My body kept trying to rid itself of food and liquid even after there was nothing left. Tears were rolling down my cheeks. I was gasping for air.

Then I felt it. The touch of Billy's hand on my back. He reached for my long hair and placed it in a hair tie. I felt a wet washcloth on the nape of my neck. "I've known this whole time," his tone was flat, "I've just been waiting for you to tell me."

I rolled away from the toilet and onto my back. His deep blue eyes didn't look angry. He was half-smiling at me with his hand on my stomach. I placed my hands over his and kept my gaze on him. "I'm so sorry, Billy. I was going to tell you on Christmas Eve. I just couldn't do it. I couldn't hurt our son." Even me saying that out loud sounded right.

Billy just sighed. He went into a long explanation of how he never wanted to hurt our kid or me and how his dad didn't understand our love. I apologized for having a crazy mother, an alcoholic father, and a dysfunctional family, but Billy didn't care about any of that. He just wanted us to be okay. We talked about packing everything and moving cross-country, but Billy had his construction company and crews. The conversation ran long and deep until I realized I had to leave for finals.

We rushed around getting all of my things together. Billy was throwing gloves, a hat, and a scarf in my direction, and everything seemed normal for a minute. He walked me to my car, and with a long hug and even longer kiss, he told me that he would talk to his father and that everything was going to be okay. He also promised me that he'd wait until after Christmas to tell them. We would be married the Sunday right after Valentine's Day anyway. I would be showing, though, and we knew what that would mean to his "perfect" father.

Billy rushed me into the car. "I've got it handled. I love you. Go!" Those were the last words I would ever hear him say to me.

I returned home after a long day of finals after a drive through sleeting rain. I was exhausted, hungry, and ready to tell Billy all about my day. I didn't notice his father's car parked next to the barn. When I went to turn the handle to go inside, the door was locked. I reached in my backpack, pulled out the key, but it didn't fit. I was confused. I knocked on the door. I could see Billy through the window, but he had his back to me. I rang the doorbell as the sleet fell harder. Billy didn't move. I turned and looked around the yard, and it was then that I saw the car.

I started screaming, "No! Billy, let me in. Let's talk this out! Come on!" I dropped my things and ran to the back of the house. The door was locked. I tried my key. The lock had been changed. I ran to the side door only to discover the same. I ran back to the front door. I knocked so hard I thought the glass would shatter. Then, I heard a voice inside of my head. That's the only way I can explain it. It told me to leave. I didn't question it.

As I ran back toward my car I noticed my things in freshly packed boxes in the shed. Not sure what to do, I packed as many of them as I could into my small Beetle and left. I was soaking wet, freezing, and in shock. My little car was also not made for the weather I was driving in. It was slipping and sliding everywhere. My head was spinning, and I was talking out loud to myself, and maybe to God, too. *How could this have happened? Why didn't Billy wait to tell his dad? What would his mother think of her soon-to-be daughter-in-law and grandson getting thrown out into a winter storm?* None of my questions were answered.

Pulling into the same gas station where all of this started, I reached for a dime and called the only person I knew would be home… my mother. I knew I would have to make her out to be the hero for this plan to work. I would have to say that she was the only person who could help me, that I had made a massive mistake by not apologizing to her for making her kick me out the last time, and that I would do better. Thankfully, for the sake of my son, it worked. I kept his existence a secret from my mother and made my way back home.

The narcissistic cycle is hard to explain to someone who has never lived it before. It involves a lot of gaslighting, seeking admiration, self-importance, criticism, emotional and physical abuse, exploiting other people for personal gain, rage, and revenge. Because of this, I knew I had to be extra careful and that I needed an exit plan and fast!

We made it through Christmas and the New Year mostly because my siblings came to visit with gifts and loads of attention directed toward my mother. This was great for me. It gave me assurance that my mother was focused on herself and not me. That ended abruptly the first week of January. Luckily for me, classes resumed at school, so I came home very late at night most days and left before she was awake. I started working as a receptionist part-time to save money for my place. I also picked up an internship position again at a local women's shelter for the battered and abused. My life was back to the way it was before Billy except for the secret I carried.

The Monday after school started back up, I arrived home and found my mother smoking a cigarette in the kitchen. "Here," she held out her pack, "Join me." She knew I wasn't smoking. This was a test. Join her or become an immediate enemy. This was the game she played since I could remember.

"I'm good, thanks, but you enjoy yours." I smiled, knowing she hated that it didn't work.

Mother stood and walked to the kitchen counter closer to me. "You don't think I know what's going on?" My stomach turned. This is how her battles always began. First, she'd come too close; then, she would lock in on her target. "Prancing around here like you own the place. With all your books, thinking you're so smart. You're such a little bitch, that's what you are, but you're nothing but a whore that no man wants in his house. Good for a fuck or two, and that's it. You're a trashy whore. That's what you are, Allyson. You little piece of shit. Not to mention how ungrateful you are and all you expect and take from me."

Did I mention that I was paying rent, buying my food, and went so far as to pay her past due electricity bill? But none of that matters to a narcissist. It's never enough. They will always find things to throw in your face. My mother is the gold medal award winner for this type of behavior. At the young age of nineteen, after years of living with her without any other family around, I had seen and heard it all from her.

I shook my head, and just like that, she raised her arm in an attempt to hit me. I grabbed her wrist, which is something I would have never done before, and told her that if she put her hands on me ever again, it would be the last thing she ever did. We held a gaze for a moment before she erupted with an evil laugh that felt like it came straight from hell.

"Go ahead, hit me, you little bitch. Let's see where that takes you. Straight to jail with the other prostitutes." I wanted to knock her head off her body, but I also didn't want to be anything like her, so I took a deep breath and stepped away. She ceased to let up. "What's that?" She pointed to my stomach. "What's going on with your fat belly, Allyson? You don't think I know that you're pregnant?! You think I'm stupid?! Billy's father called me! We both agreed that you are trash!" She was yelling, shrieking.

I placed my hands over my pregnant belly.

She ranted, "You're having a goddamn abortion! We agreed you can run back to your little whorehouse when you get rid of that trash you're carrying!" She opened her purse, pulled out her checkbook, and threw it to me. "Go!" It was like a demonic scream from a horror movie.

The gift God gave me growing up is to know when to be very still, but my motionless body even shocked me. I just stood staring at her. She wanted a reaction so desperately, and everything inside of me warned me to be still. I'm not sure I was even breathing. Mother passed me and went to her room. I stood in the kitchen for a long time. I couldn't move. I couldn't think. I couldn't do anything.

Billy's dad and my mother had made a narcissistic pact. Billy also would have known that his father called my mother. His father would have made sure of it. I hadn't heard a word from Billy. My mother decided to keep my landline telephone number, which only rang in my bedroom. There was an answering machine connected to the phone. I was sure she did this to spy on me. In any case, if Billy called, it would have been his nature to leave a message instead of simply hanging up. I didn't know this side of him and had no way of predicting his next move. While it was like him to shut down when we argued, this behavior was brand new. The truth is, though, Billy followed every command his father belted in his direction. I believed Billy would do almost anything to please his father. The betrayal and abandonment were too much for me, though; even if Billy begged his way back into my life, my trust for him was broken. In one sense, I could sympathize with the abuse, but I hated what he was doing to our child and me in another. Each day that hate grew a little deeper.

Eventually, I made my way to my bedroom, locked myself in, showered in my bathroom, and was about to climb into bed when there was a knock on my door. I dared not open it. Instead, I walked to it and spoke through the protective barrier between us. "What do you need, Mother?"

There was a long pause and then, "If you don't plan on having an abortion, don't come back to this house." Her voice was cold and flat.

My instinct guided me to take a deep breath and stay calm. I told her I was tired and asked if we could talk about it the next day. She agreed, which surprised me, but that was also her nature. There would be a massive explosion of rage and another calm between storms. In the calmness was when she would do things out of the ordinary. Her calmness often frightened me more than her rage.

The following day, I woke earlier than usual, dressed, and headed out the door when I decided to leave my mother a note. *Dear Mother, I'll leave work early today. I'll be home around eight tonight. Let's talk then. Thank you for being willing to talk this out. Love, Allyson*

I gathered the rest of my things and left. When I walked outside, it was bitter cold. Something made me go back inside for an extra scarf and a thick blanket wrapped around me as I walked our long walkway to my car. The wind was whipping hard, and my car was like an iceberg.

It was the usual day of classes, the library, my job, and I called out at the shelter so that I could talk to my mother about our next steps. It hadn't occurred to me that I was three months pregnant with no plan until that day. The only thing I was focused on was keeping my baby. A sinking feeling took over. Without Billy in my life, and with only a little bit of money saved, I would be taking on the world with a baby along for the ride. Intentionally raising my son in my mother's home brought nothing but colossal resistance. Meanwhile, my dad wasn't the best option, either. Because of my mother's abuse, he and I hadn't been as close. I didn't know him well enough to make a judgment call. My insides were shaking.

The sky was dark gray on the drive home, with a mixture of sleet and snow coming down. It was hitting hard against my windshield making it difficult to see. My wipers worked double time, and I was driving slowly to stay on slippery roads. Hardly anyone was out. I felt alone. As I continued to go, I thought about how alone I was and how awful being in the situation was turning out. While I had done everything possible to keep my son safe, and that was important to me, I was putting myself last. I wasn't so sure that I was the best option. Also, I would have to face my mother again and have 'the talk,' and that proposition made me sick to my stomach.

When I finally arrived back at my mother's house, it was just after dark, and something felt off. I climbed out of my car and walked to the door. It was locked. We rarely used the front door and knew it would be closed, so I walked to the basement door only to find it bolted. The wind picked up, and I walked quickly back up the wrought-iron steps. From the landing, I could see into the kitchen. Even though my mother's car was parked in the driveway, the lights were off. I didn't have a key to the house because we rarely locked the house. I knocked for a few minutes, but my hands quickly froze, even with gloves on them.

I stood at the door, trying to make a decision. Finally, I walked around to the front door on our covered porch and rang the bell. I waited a few minutes. Then, I knocked hard. I contemplated breaking the window but thought better of it. My whole body was shaking from the winter storm.

Back inside my car, I decided to drive to a payphone, even though my maternal grandmother lived only three doors down. My grandmother was the root of all my mother's evil. This same woman had referred to me as "the devil's spawn" just a few years before this chaos, so there was no way I would ever ask her for help.

As I was pulling out of our driveway, Norman, our next-door neighbor, was collecting the mail from his box, so I rolled down my window and asked if he'd seen my mother. Sidenote: Norman and his wife watched our house like vultures over their prey, so if she were in the house, he would know it. He hesitated for a moment, then went on to tell me that he'd seen the porch light and then the inside lights go off just a little bit before my arrival home.

"I'm sorry, Allyson," was all he could manage to say before walking back inside. He and his wife saw so much. The men coming in and out of our driveway after my mother kicked out my dad. My brief relationship with a stepfather until my mother decided he wasn't the rich man she'd conjured up in her sick mind. She threw him out as soon as she became aware that his wife hadn't left him millions of dollars in life insurance as she'd been secretly hoping. Then, my neighbors watched as I ran to school and back home after another incident with a stranger left me terrified. I shared with them only because they were genuinely concerned about me. I felt Norman knew something, but he wasn't going to tell me.

When I found a payphone, I decided to call my house, and I let the line ring until it cut me off. It had to have been twenty rings. She had disconnected the answering machine. I put the dime back in the phone and dialed the number. Snow and sleet were pounding against the glass booth. I shook, standing in the cold, waiting for her to answer the phone. It was too early for her to be asleep. She had kicked me out before for having solid boundaries, but I couldn't wrap my brain around the fact that she could kick me out knowing I was pregnant. Still, she wasn't answering the door or the phone.

Arriving back at her house, I ran to the front door this time and kicked it several times. I was screaming, "Please, open the door! It's freezing out here! Come on! Please!" Nothing. Then, just to drive her crazy, I rang the doorbell repeatedly for several minutes.

Ding-Dong. Ding-Dong. Ding-Dong

I rang it over and over again. Just to drive the point home, I kicked the front door many times as hard as possible. I'm surprised it didn't fall. My adrenaline was in high gear as I ran to the backdoor and repeated the doorbell and door-knocking charade all over again.

I knew she wasn't coming to save me, and I no longer cared. "You're a fucking bitch, mother! A cold-hearted piece of shit is what you are! I'm carrying your grandson! You'll pay for this! Karma is a bitch, you whore!" My throat burned, so I slowly walked back to my car. I climbed inside and blasted the heat.

"God, I hope you know what you're doing!" I was incensed. None of this made sense to me. Wasn't doing the right thing supposed to come with its rewards? I poured my heart out to God. I was sobbing and shaking, "I know you're guiding me to stay pregnant. I feel it, so why are you making this so hard? Why are you allowing my mother to do this? I don't understand." My sobs turned to almost violent convulsions. Snot and tears were dripping all over me. I didn't have any tissue, so I wiped my face with the sleeves of my sweater. Then it occurred to me: I didn't have any other clothes. Everything I owned was inside her house. Maybe she'd placed my clothes in garbage bags and put them somewhere.

As cold as it was, I made the rounds again to see if my clothes were anywhere. There was no sign of them. This pissed me off! I went back to the front door and banged until my knuckles bled. I didn't understand how the mother of a pregnant daughter could be in her bedroom, lying in bed, knowing her grandson was in her daughter's belly. How could she kick me out in the coldest winter on record in Atlanta? Also, to make matters worse, she knew I had nowhere to go and didn't care. All she saw was that any burden she was going to carry, any embarrassment she'd have to bear from her daughter being unwed and pregnant, was over. Her problems were solved, and mine was just beginning.

Go back to your car...NOW! the voice echoed in my head. It wasn't my voice, and it captured my full attention. I took deep breaths. Not knowing if it was the freezing temperature or impending danger, I ran to my car. Inside it was warm. I checked the locks on both sides, put my seat back, and collected myself.

I apologized to God for the awful things I had said to my mother through the door. "I don't want to be that person. I don't want to be like her. I'm just angry and hurt. Please forgive me!" Peace flooded me. Then, I heard the voice again.

Go back to school. Park in the bottom level of the garage. I sat thinking about the voice, the garage, and what I would do once I arrived there. *Go now!* The voice was male energy, and, in my mind, it was God.

I adjusted my seat, reversed my car, and headed downtown without hesitation. HOWEVER, as I was pulling out of the driveway, a light caught my eye. My mother was in my bedroom, standing at my window. I stopped hoping that she'd been asleep and didn't intend to leave me out in the cold. I stopped at the top of the driveway and waited. She was standing and staring at my car. I put my car back in drive, and when I started to pull forward, she quickly left the window and turned off my bedroom light. I waited ten minutes to see if she would open the front door or turn on the front porch light as a sign for me to return. She did neither.

She wanted me to see so that I knew it was all intentional on her part. The evil inside her was apparent, and it made me sick inside. However, I was proud of myself for not getting back out of my car and going through the whole charade again. That's what she wanted me to do. She fed off my misery and her neglect. Some wounds deep inside of her craved her dark energy. She won every time.

I put the car in reverse, pulled out of the driveway, and even though I was violently shaking from head to toe, inside and out, I did as the voice instructed me and returned to the parking garage.

Hoping and Wishing

Do you wish someone else would change so that you could feel happier?

_____

_____

Maybe you have many people you feel this way toward.

Do you have a difficult time accepting that people don't change for us?

Have you ever felt like you needed to change for someone else?

If so, how did that work out for you?

_____

_____

_____

_____

_____

Is abandonment one of your biggest fears?

_____

Would you rather stay with someone you don't want to be with than venture out on your own?

_____

Did you know that "fear of abandonment" is the number one fear of mankind? People fear being alone more than they fear death. Does that sound crazy to you?

_____

Have you ever lied – like a really big lie – in order to not be abandoned?

_____

_____

_____

If so, how did the situation turn out for you?

_____

_____

_____

_____

_____

Do you find that you experience the heavy feelings of shame and guilt (Shilt) more often than not?

If so, what do you think is causing it?

_____

_____

_____

_____

_____

If you could wave a magic wand and make the past different, what would you change?

_____

_____

_____

_____

_____

Finding the courage to change our present lives so that our future can be different is something so few people are willing to fully commit to, but when they do, they transform in ways they never believed possible.

CHAPTER FIVE

MY CAR

If I had known that my car would be my home for the next twenty-three days, I'm not sure I would have survived. While suicide only crossed my mind on the very last night of my wild adventure, there were many nights when I felt utterly hopeless and utterly ashamed. How I ended up in that situation was lost on me. I felt deserving of living in a frozen tin can and resorting to eating out of a trash can on my very last day of being homeless. The bottom line is that I believed my mother when she told me that I was worthless and unwanted by everyone. She'd said that to me so many times that it had built a neurotransmitter in my brain. I believed it and made all my decisions, meaning that I didn't ask for help, even from my own family, because I was convinced everyone would reject me.

Each day when I woke up after only two or three hours of sleep, I was so cold I thought I would die. Every morning I managed to make it to the ladies' locker room inside the campus, take a hot shower, and wash my underwear in the sink. There were hand dryers mounted on the wall, and I would dry my underwear there. I had been wearing the same clothes since I left my mother's house. Surely everyone could tell. I managed to scrape together enough money from my car to purchase deodorant at a nearby gas station. My meal card at school allowed for one meal a day, so that's how I was eating. It wasn't a lot of food, but better than nothing. I quit my job because I used all the gasoline in my car to stay warm. With no money for bus fare, and a job that wasn't within walking distance, this only deflated me more. The one thing keeping me sane was school.

I walked into class one day and on the board was a graph. At the top was a circle, and inside the circle were the words, "Things happen." Directly under that was another circle with the words, "You think, You feel." Then, two circles were directly underneath that, one on the left and another on the right. To the left, the word inside the circle read, "React," and in the other circle, "Respond." The bottom circle also contained the words, "Real life." Many years later, Brooke Castillo would simplify this method, but in 1985 I had never seen anything remotely close to how the brain processes what's happening outside the circumstances. My chain of recent events was slowly mounting into a pile of very unmanageable days and nights. I was reaching the end of my rope. My belly was also rapidly outgrowing the only sweater I owned.

As the days went on, we learned that as soon as an outside circumstance happens, our brain is triggered either with happy thoughts or ones that provoke sadness, anger, or fear. We go into flight, fight, or freeze if we think of fear predominantly. Each of us has a fear response that rules our body. The more past trauma we've lived through, the more likely we will go into a fear response and stay there. Even though this had all been explained to me in my short stint in therapy, I was learning it differently now. It all made sense. However, no one talked about the spiritual aspect that comes into play when you're faced with a life-or-death situation or what feels like it could be the end-of-life decision.

Each night in my car, I would use the model we learned to understand all the decisions I made about my pregnancy. The part that was missing was God's intervention. It's the only way I could explain the sign at church that day with Billy and the voice in my head. I also heard that voice daily since I arrived at my new residence's school parking garage. Every day, it would direct me to go inside, shower, drink lots of water, and go to class.

On one particular day, I was checking out books at the school library when the librarian asked if I was okay. This was the first time anyone had shown any concern toward me. You would think I would have a lot of friends at school, but most of the students were adults returning to college for career purposes. I was younger than many people in my class, and without dorms at school, it was a pretty much come-to-class-and-go-home type of atmosphere. I dropped out of my study group because, again, I didn't have a car with gasoline to get me there. Without being able to explain why I left without blowing my cover that I was living on campus in my car, I made up some lame story. It appeared that everyone in the group assumed I didn't like them because after I left, they all stopped talking to me. I didn't have the energy to put in restoring the relationships. So, the librarian noticed my situation and said something that meant the world to me. I remember just nodding and fighting back the tears. Gathering my things, I walked to my car. It was day nineteen when this happened. It was also a Friday, which meant the campus would be mostly empty the next day. It also meant no food for two days. I hated the weekends.

Monday arrived. I went straight to the dining hall. The workers were there, and I remember lying about having a blood sugar issue. One of the ladies who was busy cutting up vegetables looked down at my belly. "Looks like you got a baby issue, too." She smiled at me. I managed to smile back. Maybe she noticed how thin I was in every other part of my body or how dark the circles were underneath my eyes. She made me sit down at a table in the back of the kitchen while she scrambled eggs, made French toast, and put grapes on the plate, too. I choked back tears as I scarfed down the feast. She sat with me, and I could see so many questions in her eyes. She left and came back with chocolate milk, cereal, raisins, and strawberries, "Here, eat some more." I poured the chocolate milk over the cereal, added what was left of the raisins, and put whole strawberries in the bowl, too. The cereal was gone within just a couple of minutes. I was packed – like really full. My belly was tight. I stood, and before I left, I asked the earth angel if I could hug her. My hug was so tight! I loved her so much for her caring heart, warm smile, kind eyes, and for feeding my son and me. Her questions couldn't be contained, "Are you a student here?"

"I am."

"You live close by?" She gave me a warm smile.

"I do."

"You in trouble? You know, are you being abused or anything?" We locked eyes.

"Not anymore." I gave her a genuine smile. She smiled and patted me on my shoulder, "When you get hungry, you come looking for me, ya hear?"

"Thank you," I whispered and left with her eyes watching every step I took. I looked upward, *Thank you. I needed that angel.* I heard the voice inside my head again. *I know.*

I was the first person to arrive at my Psych class that day. The teacher who'd taught us the model about outside circumstances wasn't there and in her place was a man wearing a bowtie. He'd taught us a few weeks before and again just over the week before. I had also seen him in the library a few times and had interrupted him to ask questions about neurotransmitters in the brain. This man was intelligent and on his game.

On his desk was a radio blaring breaking news, "The Inauguration of President Ronald Reagan will take place in the Capitol Rotunda as record temperatures hit Washington, D.C. In local news, Atlanta braces for more record-breaking temperatures. Last night, Atlanta experienced its coldest night in history at a negative 10 degrees. That wasn't the windchill, folks; that was our actual temperature." I felt my body shiver. The only reason I was alive, I felt, is because I found five heavy towels and three fairly thick blankets in the locker room on different days. In addition to wanting to conceal myself in my car, the combination of towels and blankets was keeping me alive. I was thankful that I parked my car as the voice had instructed. My car was on the bottom floor, tucked away in the middle of two concrete pillars and a wall. This way, there was no wind or outside cold whipping through my car. While it was cold and I hadn't had a natural sleep in three weeks, I considered myself lucky.

The substitute kept looking at me during class. Every time I looked up, I caught him looking at me. Later that day, I was in the library, and he'd approached me to see if I had any questions about his lecture or anything else. It was genuine, and I took advantage of it. So as not to disturb the other people in the library, we went back to the classroom, where he demonstrated different mind models on the board. I was excelling, and it felt great for the first time in a while. As we were going through scenarios, I suddenly felt butterflies in my stomach. This was my son. Even though I'd never thought it before, I immediately knew the feeling was the first movement of my child. My hand instinctively landed on my belly.

"How far along are you?" My professor smiled.

"I'm not exactly sure, but I think about four months."

He went on to tell me how his wife knew she was pregnant with their three sons right away and how she would run across the room and grab his hand to feel the movement, too. My mind flashed to that first night with Billy when we were so happy about this baby. My mentor must have sensed my sadness. "But you don't want to hear about me." He immediately returned to the board, where we spent another two hours going over the lessons.

Then, the janitor opened the door. "We are closing up early tonight to get you kids home. The cold is unreal." I felt fear rush in. I was confident that I had enough blankets, but I wasn't positive. We all bid our farewells, and I headed to my car.

Once inside, I started crying, *God, please, please, please, keep us safe and alive!* I was wailing. *I don't want to die.* I thought about calling my older sister, but she lived a state away. I had no gas, and even if she drove to get me, there was school. I didn't want to quit school. My dad crossed my mind, but our relationship wasn't the greatest. It was all on me and had been on me since the age of ten. I pumped myself up that I had this and that I would be okay. After all, I had eaten breakfast *and* lunch that day. Life was good.

A few hours in, I woke up in pain. While I was underneath a bunch of material, nothing matched the frozen state of that garage. I looked at my hands, and they were red. I couldn't feel my toes. I curled my body as tight as I could, which wasn't easy in the backseat of the Beetle. I tucked myself tightly into the seat, pushing all edges of blankets and towels into every possible nook and cranny. I was breathing warm air into my hands when the realization that I could die hit me. I was staring into the blackness around me. *I saved my son, and now we are going to die. They are going to find us frozen to death. Here. At school. Inside my car.* I started apologizing to him for being in the situation, for no prenatal care, for Billy and Billy's dad. I apologized on behalf of my parents and grandparents. I told him how much I loved him. Then, I heard the voice. *Do it again, Allyson.*

A few weeks earlier, that same instructor who'd helped me in the library gave me a copy of *Think and Grow Rich* by Napoleon Hill. In the book, the author talks about visualization as the key to what we want in life. But more than that, we have to desire something so much that it begins building a new belief system within us. Every night since he gifted me the book, I had been visualizing and desiring to be in a warm room, with warm tea on the nightstand, along with flannel pajamas, thick socks, and a doctor's appointment on a wall calendar I could see from the bed. I also imagined blue curtains with tiny purple flowers dressing the window. I could see the street light coming in the window, lighting up the room a few nights. I walked over and closed the curtains, climbed back into bed, and slept deeply.

Now, I was being instructed to do it again. I didn't feel like it. I certainly wasn't desiring it at the moment. All I could think was that I was going to freeze to death. Also, I was so hungry. On my way to my car, I heard that same voice tell me to go and look in a trash can that was in the hallway by the exit. The janitor was making everyone leave in a hurry, and inside the trashcan lay an uneaten sandwich in a zip lock bag along with an unopened bag of potato chips. I reached in and took it. No one was around, but I still felt so small and sad. I didn't deserve to be eating from a trash can. I put my hand out from under the covers and picked up the sandwich on my floorboard. Under the covers, I removed it from its bag and started eating. It tasted so good.

I closed my eyes. There it was. The bedroom. The bed. The warmth. The curtains. The pajamas. The socks. The calendar. I took another bite of the sandwich. I thought about eating it while sitting in that bed as I chewed. I was safe. I was peaceful. I desired this. I was there.

Just then, there was a knock on my window. It snapped me back to reality. Of course, my windows were all fogged from my breathing, but I hoped whoever it was would just go away.

"Allyson, open the door." It was my teacher! Crap! My cover was blown.

As always, it took me a minute to maneuver the covers, my seat, and make my way to the door handle. I slowly opened the door, climbed out, and wrapped whatever I could grab around me. As soon as I exited my car, my teacher told me to follow him home. "The temperature is drastically dropping, Allyson; you'll freeze here. I don't know what's going on, and I don't care, but you can't stay here."

I studied his face. He continued, "Look, my wife knows I came to get you. She's the one who insisted after I told her that I thought you were living in your car." He wanted me to follow him, but I explained that my car was out of gas from trying to stay warm. So, he grabbed all of my stuff from my car, put it in the cab of his pickup truck, and motioned for me to climb in. "If I go back home without you, my wife won't be happy."

On the way to his home, it was made clear that my stay was only for a few days while we figured out a place for me to stay until, at least, my son was born. He was nervous but more about my health than anything. He was firing many questions at me about prenatal care, my parents, the baby's father, and my plans. I grew dizzy just answering him. He apologized, and we shared a good laugh. What I remember most about that ride was the heat from the vents. I held my hands up to them, and my feet were also getting a blast from the lower vents. I hadn't been that happy to ride in a car ever.

I closed my eyes and silently thanked God. He guided me out of the clinic, then to lie to Billy, then to my mother's house, then to the garage, then to this teacher, and now to warmth and safety. God was very real to me at that moment.

When we arrived at the house, his wife stood at a glass storm door waiting for us. She hugged me the second she met me. I towered over her, but she managed to hug my neck and not let go.

Her very first words to me were, "You're safe here."

I felt it. She showed me to my room, and as soon as she turned on the light, I saw them. On either side of the window were purple curtains with tiny blue flowers.

A Special Gift from Allyson

Now that you have your copy of *The Spiritual Journey: The Part No One Talks About*, you are on your way to understanding that even when the world seems to be falling apart, you are a powerful manifestor! Plus ... I hope my story is helping you understand how much you are loved by the Universe and that perfection is not expected of you in order to build the life you want to live.

You'll also receive the special bonus I created to add to your toolkit ... **The Reset**, which is a guided meditation for you to connect with your angels, guides, and masters so that you can wipe your emotional slate clean and continue your journey feeling renewed.

There's so much confusing information out there about spirituality and manifesting. When you finish this book you'll be armed with what you need to know about creating the life your heart desires without having to do it perfectly or be perfect.

While this meditation is offered for sale, just go to the link below and tell us where to send it.

https://www.allysonroberts.com/resetmeditation

The sooner you know how to begin visualizing and attracting everything you want into your life, the better your chances of no longer attracting the things you *don't want!*

I'm in your corner. Let me know if I can help further.

Here's to manifesting your best life!

Best,

Allyson

CHAPTER SIX

DECISIONS

The following day, after a long sleep in a soft bed and a very hot shower, I found myself wearing the softest pajamas imaginable. I made my way to the kitchen. It was late, and I had missed class. While I felt panicked in one sense, the other part of me didn't care.

Beth, the professor's wife, was in the kitchen waiting for me. "Good morning, Allyson." Her smile was infectious.

I smiled back at her, "Hi, um…can I give you a hug?" She opened her arms to receive me. It was a genuine embrace, and I finally felt safe.

We sat down, and she poured hot tea for us both. Through the kitchen window, I saw ice everywhere. Classes had been canceled all over Atlanta. I hadn't missed anything after all. Ralph, my teacher, was still asleep. The house was so quiet, and we both embraced the comforting silence. Neither of us spoke as we watched the cardinals on the feeders on the back porch. I closed my eyes and tried not to think about Billy. We had sat on the porch together so many mornings with our coffee watching the birds feed and the cows graze. I felt alone but grateful, and it was a sensation I had come to know very well.

"I need to schedule a doctor's appointment," I interrupted the silence.

"We wanted to talk to you about that this morning," Ralph was behind me. He'd entered so quietly. He smiled at me, then continued, "Good morning."

"Good morning." We exchanged a knowing look, but I said it anyway. "I can't thank you enough for letting me come here last night. I don't think I would have survived another night in my car."

I don't remember what was said after that because my thoughts went straight to my car that was still parked in the garage. My monthly parking pass would expire soon, I didn't have gas to put in the tank, and I wasn't even sure it would start at this point.

They pulled me back into the conversation. Ralph had a friend who was going to pick up my car. Since we weren't sure yet where I would be staying, I was assured that his friend would keep my car at his shop. That piece of my complicated puzzle was solved almost immediately. Then, instantly as if on cue, shame seeped in. *Who was I to be receiving this help? My own family couldn't help me, so why should these strangers care?*

My mother's voice was dominating my headspace. I could hear all the evil things she constantly said to me. *You're pathetic. You can't do anything right. No one likes you. You're a burden.*

One minute, I was fully engaged in the conversation, and the very next second, I was in my mother's hell. I could see lips moving, but I had no concept of what was said. I would find out later that this is a symptom of PTSD.

Ralph decided we should get dressed and have lunch at a local barbeque place since it was the only place open in the storm. Beth laid out some of her clothes for me to wear. There are no words to describe the feeling of putting on different clothes after three weeks of wearing the same thing twenty-four hours a day. It was a sweatsuit, and it fit perfectly. She also gave me undergarments, a long-sleeve t-shirt, fresh socks, and while I was sleeping, she'd washed my tennis shoes. I was brand new in that I felt clean and fresh, and my dignity was restored.

Everyone knew each other at the restaurant. Ralph and Beth greeted basically everyone in there. I was introduced to every person that came through the door. I must have heard, "This is our friend, Allyson," a dozen times. It was crowded and cozy with a massive fire in the wood-burning fireplace. The smell of barbecue permeated the room. At last, I felt safe, accepted, and warm.

There wasn't much privacy, so conversation was kept to Beth's work as an artist, Ralph's "real" job as a marketing consultant, and their immediate goals. We also talked about their grown sons, the desire for grandchildren, and their time dog-sitting for their kids. We laughed until we cried at some stories about the "grand-dogs." My heart was filled with peace.

All good things must come to an end, and when we arrived back at their house, it was time for serious deliberation about my circumstances. Ralph led most of the conversation, and it was clear to me that he and Beth were already in communication with outside agencies, counselors, and lawyers.

At first, Ralph offered to speak with Billy and Billy's father to see if he could help mend fences and get us back on track to be married in February, which was only a few weeks away. After explaining to him how racist Billy's father was and how a black man showing up or even calling would only result in Ralph being insulted, he backed away from that idea. Talking about the senior members of the family's racism also opened my eyes to the fact that I didn't want to be in any part of their lives anymore. I had been so transfixed on Billy that I hadn't stopped to think about everything I would be marrying into. I shared that with Ralph and Beth, and Beth fully understood because as a white woman herself, especially in the 1970s when she'd met Ralph, both families struggled with their interracial marriage.

Beth was candid, "Allyson, instead of us trying to lay the pavers for your next steps, tell us what you want."

I then shared everything leading up to living in my car, from working in the diner, getting my first internship, therapy, meeting Billy, leaving that situation, to being homeless. Beth squeezed my hands as I walked them through the abortion clinic details. Tears were running down her face. Ralph stood and started pacing. He seemed to be in deep thought as I shared about the abuse my siblings and I suffered as children, how the therapist I was seeing suspected my mother of clinical narcissism and my father of codependence, to all of us being separated now and barely speaking.

"My God," I heard Beth say under her breath.

The room went silent again for a while. Beth remained still and held my hands. Ralph stood in one place staring out the window, and my eyes fixed on a stain on their kitchen table that kind of resembled Mona Lisa. That image carried me to thoughts of traveling around the world, seeing things in person that I had only seen in textbooks, and being in the same spaces as Michelangelo, Shakespeare, and Mary Magdalene. The chance to feel their energy and breathe the same air they breathed seemed heavenly.

Ralph snapped me back to reality, "Allyson, thank you for sharing everything you did with us, but Beth is right. You need to guide us to what it is you want. We will help you, but you can't stay here much longer because our son comes back to live with us next weekend. I'm sorry."

"Please don't apologize," I answered.

I shared how I had taken *Think and Grow Rich* seriously but that I was only thinking about being warm. I shared with them about seeing the same curtains hanging in their guestroom in my vision in my car. They were both intrigued. I was convinced that I didn't know what to do next, except that I needed to start prenatal care.

Ralph invited me to follow him to his office. There on the wall was a chalkboard, and he wrote three columns: *Keep the Baby, Give the baby to Billy*, and *Adoption to Strangers.*

Picking up the eraser, I immediately erased the option to give the baby to Billy. That wasn't realistic, and after realizing how toxic his family was, I didn't want my son influenced by them. I also didn't want my son growing up feeling like abusing and abandoning people was acceptable behavior. We pored over all the details of the other options. I had already secretly been contemplating adoption, as painful as it was to even think about.

Beth was pushing for me to keep the baby and had a valid argument for each point I made about not having a place to live, a reliable car, a job, or family to help support me. Ralph would occasionally chime in to tell me about Section 8 housing, food stamps, Medicaid, child support, and other free services.

Something in my gut was directing me toward adoption. By the end of the day, that was the decision. Ralph and Beth both agreed that I should sleep on it. But first, Beth took me into their attic, where she had boxes of maternity clothes her daughter-in-law had asked her to take and donate. She had never made it to Goodwill, so we went through the boxes together. I ended up with several pieces that fit well and could be mixed and matched with other items. She also had shoes that fit, a maternity coat, and matching galoshes.

Beth could sense my discomfort in accepting her generosity. "It's okay; this is what she wanted me to do with these. Please take them, wear them, and enjoy them. Otherwise, you're going to be in my sweatsuit every day!" It felt good to laugh and I hugged the clothes to my body tightly.

The following day, I woke early and went to school. I headed straight for the parking garage only to find the space empty. Even though it was freezing, I stood there in a dreamlike trance. How had I survived? Being back in that space, the cold was overwhelming. Even with all the towels and blankets over me, I should have died. Not to mention constantly being hungry. I wiped the tears on my cheeks and walked to my first class. It felt good to be in cute maternity clothes. Everyone commented on my showing belly and said they had no idea I was pregnant. For the first time, I felt seen at school.

Later that day, I had my first doctor's appointment. The shame of not receiving care flooded in when the nurse asked how far along I was and then, with an attitude, asked why I had waited so long. She seemed unphased when I explained that I was homeless and reminded me that the baby was now my priority. When I explained to her that I had been to an abortion clinic and changed my mind, she rolled her eyes. This was not going to be the place walking me through an adoption process. I didn't bother telling her my plans for adoption because I didn't want to know her response.

The doctor was colder than the nurse. He examined me, threw a bottle of prenatal vitamins at me from across the room, told me to start gaining weight and congratulated me for not smoking. He also said that I wasn't as far along in my pregnancy as I'd thought. "You're due July 20th, congrats." Then, he left the room.

A different nurse was still in the room with me. She was young, pretty, and doe-eyed. I burst into tears. From start to finish, I felt humiliated. I also thought the baby was due in June, not July, and that threw me. I also heard his heartbeat for the first time during the appointment, and when that had brought me to tears, no one reached for my hand to comfort me. I also wanted an ultrasound that day, but it was refused because I didn't have insurance. Ralph and Beth covered my first visit from a fund at their church.

On the bus back to my temporary home, I cried the whole way. People were staring at me, and I didn't care. It wasn't about them; this was about my broken heart. It was shattered. I felt flawed. My plans felt wasted. How did I end up here? Why did God let this happen? I took every birth control pill on time. I did my part. Yet, here I was, still homeless, still pregnant, still ashamed, still alone, and still devastated. I had been in survival mode living in my car. I gave myself no time to feel anything except motivated to live. Now with a safety net, however temporary, I was falling apart inside. I needed help that only my therapist could give me.

Back at the house, I shared my experience at the doctor's office with my new friends, who were now like family. Ralph was pissed, but Beth didn't seem that shocked. I told them that I would call my therapist and schedule an appointment. Ralph asked how I would pay for it, and I hadn't even thought about it. Not from a place of irresponsibility but more from an area of numbness. He had an idea.

While I was at class that day, they reached out to Catholic Social Services about their adoption program. Their priest suggested that I receive their services and assured Ralph and Beth that I didn't have to be a Catholic. They had already visited and had a packet ready for me when I got home. We explored each step, and Ralph explained the parts I didn't understand.

A nun on staff interviewed me, and if accepted, they would place me in their Unwed Mothers program. This would require me to live with a host family and receive prenatal care, while attending counseling and Catholic Mass weekly, meeting with a support group, and then ultimately placing my son for adoption. My care would be covered, but I would receive no monetary compensation. I could still attend school and work if I chose to do so. The plan seemed straightforward.

I was interrogated by four nuns and two priests a few days later. They would probably disagree that they were rude and intimidating, but I felt judged.

"Allyson, tell us about your drug use," asked a nun wearing a full habit.

"I don't use drugs. Never have," I said with a very pissed-off tone.

"I see," she replied, with the doubt floating in the air.

A priest stared at me, "What about alcohol? We will need to know those details."

"I drank in high school. I haven't touched liquor in over a year." I could feel the tears of frustration forming.

Still, another priest chimed in, "Is the father of this baby, if you know who the father is, a white man?"

"Who the fuck cares what race the father is? I have a beautiful baby growing inside of me that needs a loving and caring home." I stood, "The father was my fiancé! He wanted me to abort our child to cover up any family embarrassment, God forbid. His father called me a whore. My mother wanted me to abort my pregnancy. I'm pro-choice, by the way! If *that* matters. I'm not going to sit here and take your judgment, your condescending tones. You either have a family for this baby, or you don't, but either way, my life matters! His life matters! I won't be treated like shit, and he *definitely* won't be treated like shit! So, make up your mind, and let me know. I'm going home." Ralph was waiting in the lobby, and I was hysterical when I reached him.

"Hey, hey, hey," Ralph hugged me, "What in the world happened there?"

I asked him if we could please leave. Then, one of the nuns who hadn't spoken while I was in the interrogation room came hurrying toward us. She apologized profusely, explaining that most unwed mothers they assisted were struggling with addiction, mental illness, or the ability to take care of themselves. She explained that her experience was very different, and she found that most of her cases were young women just like me… jilted.

"I'm Sister Mary," the nun gave me a warm smile.

My gut instinct told me to keep up a wall. I didn't like her. She could have come to my rescue in front of her cold and racist coworkers, but instead, she allowed them to treat me like a second-class citizen.

"Allyson, please come back to my office. I will handle your case from here. You won't have to speak with those people again. How does that sound?" Sister Mary was begging me at this point.

Ralph asked for a few minutes alone with me. He was mortified and disappointed. He apologized to me and assured me that I didn't need to go through with the appointment if I was uncomfortable. After several minutes of him and I deliberating back and forth and weighing all the options, I decided to give Sister Mary another chance.

When she heard my decision, the smile on her face was soft and genuine. I felt her hand on my back as she walked me toward her office. I saw two black file cabinets, a gentrified picture of Jesus on the wall with blonde hair and blue eyes, a single desk, and two chairs. It was cold and uninviting. Doubt flooded my brain.

Sister Mary looked deeply into my eyes, "Allyson, no matter how you feel right now, this path you are choosing is going to be a tough one. It's a decision that will stay with you the rest of your life – either way. If you choose to parent this child, they will be with you until you take your last breath. If you choose adoption, this child will be in your heart until you take your last breath. You are going to feel upset. You're going to question, doubt, second guess, and those thoughts will cause you to feel all sorts of emotions. Get used to it. You've chosen a challenging road, but if you feel good about your decision, then it's the best one no matter how difficult."

She turned back to go through a stack of papers on her desk. I looked out the window to the Atlanta skyline. It was gorgeous as it rested against a crystal blue sky. The sun was beaming down, reflecting off the glass on almost all of the buildings. I could see the parking garage where I lived those three long weeks.

"I made the right decision," I heard myself say confidently. "That I'm sure of, but this," the tears came again, "this is not how I thought I would feel, and what just happened to me is not how I expected to be treated."

Sister Mary just looked at me. She wanted to respond, but instead she explained the paperwork in front of me. There were pages of rules. No sex. No boys. No smoking. No drugs. No alcohol. No loud music. No parties. Then there were curfews and restrictions about family visits – not that I was expecting anyone to come see me. I was given stringent guidelines with even stricter consequences. My stomach turned. It wasn't that I was planning on having sex with strange boys or harming my body or my son's body with substance abuse or smoking. It was more that assumptions were being made and once again shame washed over me.

It triggered me, also, because my mother assumed I slept with every boy I knew. She constantly accused me of having sex with everyone. Now I know it was merely a projection of everything she was doing, but at the time it hurt. It added to a mountain of shame inflicted by her since the day I came into the world. My mother's lack of love, empathy and care drove me into the arms of men who refused to stand up for me, care for me, empathize with me, or love me. In my early adulthood I couldn't see the patterns, but as life opened new opportunities for me to heal and know the truth, I finally came to realize that the shame wasn't mine to carry. Only then could I move my life in a different direction.

At the end of that day with Sister Mary, I had come to understand how I would be judged the rest of my life for whatever decision I made. What other people thought mattered so much to me after nineteen years of marinating in shame. One side of me could tell a person how I felt without holding back, but then I would replay it in my mind like a broken reel, second-guessing myself and haunted by guilt. Another side of me would freeze when I was triggered, allowing me to stay in the line of fire with insults being thrown at me. Then, I would play that scene repeatedly in my head and sink into a state of guilt. It was a vicious, anxiety-inducing, never ending cycle.

On the ride back to Ralph and Beth's home, I was told it would be my last night staying with them. I wish I had known it would also be the last time I ever saw either one of them. A few months after my son was born, they moved out of state without giving me a forwarding address. For whatever reason, instead of forwarding their old landline to their new number, they simply disconnected it. Years later, I find out that Ralph was in financial trouble from a family business that went bankrupt. But, still, it stung when they deserted me. I thought our relationship was much more profound. When I talked to my therapist about it, she said that sometimes people help others to try to heal themselves. Still, together they saved my life and my son's life. The abrupt ending only added to my feeling that something was innately wrong with me, and that whatever it was made me unworthy of love.

The next day, a man who I had never seen before pulled into the driveway and introduced himself as a volunteer with Catholic Social Services. Ralph and Beth gifted me with two suitcases and more clothes to add to the ones Beth had already given me. The suitcases were full, and Ralph carried them to the car. Ralph shook hands with the driver and told him to take good care of me. Beth hugged me for an extended time until the stranger said we needed to go. As we pulled out of the driveway, I rolled down my window and blew kisses. They caught them, and Beth placed her hand on her heart.

Earth Angels

Have you ever encountered someone and instinctively knew that you were in the presence of an angel?

Yes? _____ No?_____ I don't know _____

Has someone you barely know ever helped you through something serious? (Examples are hospice worker, teacher, soldier, fireman)

Yes? _____ No? _____ I don't know _____

Looking back, what were the special qualities of the person who helped you?

_____

_____

_____

_____

_____

If you're honest with yourself, are you waiting to be rescued? If you're not sure how to answer this question, waiting to be rescued looks like this...

1. Believing the bullshit stories you tell yourself about how horrible you are because of your past.
2. Your perception of the world is a negative one.
3. You have serious money issues but refuse to look at them or do anything about them.
4. You strive for perfection.
5. You are quick to "fall in love."
6. Your expectations are too high.
7. You worry (a lot!).
8. You hold grudges against yourself and others.

9. You don't trust (yourself, others, God).

10. You're marinated in Shame and Guilt (SHILT™).

If the above list resonates with you, it's okay. Awareness is a beautiful thing. We can't heal what we don't know.

Light a candle, wrap yourself in a blanket or sit in the sun (or both), and reflect on the above list. When we wait for someone else to:

- Earn the money
- Be nice
- Change for the better
- Stop doing the thing you hate
- Start doing the thing you beg for...

...we are turning our power over to them. It hurts and it's completely unnecessary. You have everything you need right inside of you and it's just waiting to be discovered. You've got this!

CHAPTER SEVEN

LOST

When the stranger pulled into a street just around the corner from the hospital where I had been born, I knew immediately that my son would be born there. I knew this part of town well because it wasn't far from my mother's house. At least Ralph's home was on the other side of Atlanta, which gave me comfort knowing I was an hour away from my personal hell. I wasn't sure this home would work for me.

We walked up a short flight of stairs to the front door, and a woman opened the door before we rang the bell. I liked that she seemed eager to meet me. Behind her stood two children: a little girl around the age of eight with long strawberry blonde hair and a huge smile, and next to her, a little boy around five with thick black hair and big cheeks, wearing a superhero cape. They both started talking to me at once, begging me to come inside and sharing pictures they had drawn.

I sat on the couch while they told me all about their house, rooms, and backyard. Then the little girl took my hand and showed me to my room. I immediately loved it. It was the size of a living room, except it had a bed, dresser, and built-in benches by a large window. The room had its own bathroom, and I had privacy because it was above the garage. Every doubt I felt when we first arrived quickly vanished. This felt like home.

After I settled in, I was invited to have dinner with the family, something I hadn't experienced in a very long time. Liam, the husband, arrived home just in time to join the rest of us. While we enjoyed dinner, the kids asked me dozens of questions, and even though it was a lot to take in, I loved their enthusiasm and curiosity.

Later that night, Lisa and I shared tea, and she also had a lot of questions. I smiled inside, seeing how her children mimicked her zest for life and her natural love of people. The difference between this family's questions and the ones the nuns and priests had asked me was the lack of judgment. Their goal was to get to know the unwed mom who'd landed in their home through their generosity. My heart was open, and I shared it all. We shared into the wee hours of the morning, another experience I missed.

The following day I caught the bus for class, and on my way, I thought about my car. I made a note to ask Ralph about it. When I arrived at the course, though, our regular teacher greeted me as she was back from maternity leave. It surprised me that Ralph hadn't told me, but we also had a lot going on.

When I arrived back at Lisa's, I called Ralph to ask him about my car. He gave me the number to his friend's garage, and when I called it, the number was temporarily disconnected, meaning the telephone bill hadn't been paid. I called Ralph back right away only to get the answering machine with a message he and Beth recorded: "*This is Ralph. This is Beth. Please leave us a message, and we will call you back when we can.*" I chose not to leave a message.

A few weeks later, Liam drove me to the garage to inquire about my car. When we pulled into the parking lot, the building was boarded up, and there wasn't a car in sight. I slowly exited the car. Ralph and I had visited the garage many times before, each time we pulled into the garage, my car was always in the parking lot. This time, however, it was gone. I couldn't believe it. I walked over to where it was parked previously and stood in the space. It was the last thing I'd owned that was mine. Everything that meant something to me was slipping away. My car was my freedom. It was a huge part of saving my life while sheltering me. Also, my dad had given me the car for my seventeenth birthday.

Liam accessed a payphone adjacent to the parking lot. I guessed he was calling Lisa to tell her what was happening. Meanwhile, I sat down in the parking spot and stared at the boarded-up building. Maybe this was why Ralph wasn't answering my calls. Beth was also distant the times we did talk. I knew Ralph had invested money in the towing service for the garage, but that's all he shared with me.

I felt someone behind me, and it was Liam. Even though he was wearing dress pants, he didn't seem to care as he took place next to me on the pavement. "I called information and got Ralph's number. He picked up. He didn't want to talk to me at first, but he finally told me that they hauled your car to a junkyard, Allyson. He said it was too costly to fix and not worth the money it would take to make it drivable."

I felt faint. *Why hadn't anyone told me? How could they decide that without consulting with me? How had they junked it without the title? When did they do it? Who had made the decision?* Those thoughts swirled around me as Liam kept talking. I didn't hear anything he said except one sentence.

"Ralph didn't have the heart to tell you," Liam's voice cracked. That was all I managed to hear.

The sun was setting, and we weren't in the best part of town. We needed to leave, but I was having a hard time breaking myself away from nothing. There was no hope left for me in that parking lot, but I didn't want to drive away and leave it behind. It made no sense to me—none of it made sense.

"I can't leave," I started to cry. "Do you know how much I've lost? Do you have any idea what's been taken from me?" Liam shook his head. He was the silent type.

I continued, "I lost my sisters first, then my dad and brother moved out, and my dad fought for custody but my mother threatened me, so I told a jury I wanted to live with her, but it was a lie." My tears turned to sobs, "Then I lost my mother, well, I've never really had a mother, but after the divorce, she was *never* home. She also stopped parenting me. She didn't give me anything I needed, from food to school supplies. Nothing. My dad and I have fought so hard to have some type of relationship, but it's more complicated than words can say because he drinks, and he doesn't even know I'm pregnant." I could barely get the words out. "Now my car is gone! It's gone, Liam. They stole it from me!"

The situation was way out of Liam's comfort zone. He had no clue how to handle my hysteria, and it was only getting darker by the minute. We needed to be already gone, but I was planted. I sobbed and sobbed and sobbed. The truth is I was grieving for my past but also my future. I knew I needed to place my son for adoption, but no part of me wanted to say goodbye to him. With my car being taken from me, I finally allowed myself to cry without fighting the tears. I cried for Billy, and my animals back at the farm, and my mom's cruelty, and the humiliation and fear of living in a parking garage, eating out of a trash can, and peeing into an open drain in the cold. I sobbed over my family and how messed up it was. I was lost.

Finally, Liam convinced me to get back into his car. Lisa was waiting on us with dinner, too, and the kids would worry if we weren't home soon. We stopped at a McDonald's to pick up French fries to go with Lisa's grilled burgers and I took the opportunity to wash my face. When I looked in the mirror, the sadness staring back at me shocked me. I had never seen myself look so empty. I didn't try to fight it. I was exhausted.

The next day in therapy, I poured it all out to Sally, my newly assigned counselor. She listened intently without interrupting me. This was new for me. At one point, I wasn't sure she was listening, and she must have caught on because she immediately reiterated something I shared a few moments before, and I instantly felt validated. She told me that I wouldn't be cured in a day, week, or month, but that I could feel better day by day if I allowed myself to stay in acceptance and awareness. This was easier said than done.

Even though I had never experienced it before, I directed my emotions toward food in the weeks to follow. I couldn't get enough to eat. The family I was staying with was so kind about it, too. They didn't question my dozens of daily trips to the kitchen. I slowly realized that I was eating even when I wasn't hungry.

At my first doctor's visit, the nurse's first task was to weigh me. The balance beam scale maxed out at 150 on the bottom half. I had never weighed more than 135 pounds my entire life. When the bottom maxed out at 150, and the nurse started moving the marker above it, I felt my face flush. She stopped at the 15-pound marker.

"One hundred and sixty-five pounds. How far along are you?"

I shrugged my shoulders, "I think I'm five months pregnant. This is only my second visit."

The nurse gave me a disapproving look, "Is this your first child?"

I felt myself start to tear up, "Yes, and I was living in my car doing the best I could. I'm with a family now through Catholic Social Services. I'm probably going to place the baby for adoption."

A woman who was sitting in a chair next to the scale scoffed at me under her breath, "Wow."

"How much did you weigh before you got pregnant?" the nurse continued while I was still standing on the scale.

"One hundred and thirty pounds, I think," I replied sheepishly. I wanted to run and hide.

"Follow me," the nurse turned and started walking down a long hallway filled with closed doors. Each door had colored tags above it with hinges. Some indicated red, while others were blue. When we got to my exam room, she pulled the red tag. I had no idea what it meant, but it felt like I was a big problem.

"Undress from the waist down. The doctor will be here shortly," the nurse ordered.

"I would rather stay dressed since I've never met him before. I'll do my exam today, but I want to meet him before I get naked if that's okay," I surprised myself with a healthy boundary.

The nurse smiled at me, understanding my request, and agreed that it would be okay to break protocol.

When Dr. Moussakhani came into the room, I immediately felt safe. He was pure joy. He explained so much to me about gestational diabetes, nutrition, exercise, breathing exercises, and vitamins during my visit. After I shared with him everything I had been through, he asked if he could hug me. It was the warmest embrace I had felt in a very long time. We skipped the initial exam that day, which made me respect and love him even more. He scheduled me for the following week, and that is how my relationship started with this loving and caring doctor.

I tried to do everything Dr. Moussakhani instructed, following his orders, including reducing my calories. The struggle was real, and I found myself gaining more and more weight. While I knew it was unhealthy, the thought of having to say goodbye to the little person growing inside of me was devastating.

I stepped away from school. It wasn't working, and my mind was going a little crazy. During one of my walks in the neighborhood, I started a conversation with a woman walking three dogs. They were beautiful, and I wanted to pet them. She told me that she managed a nearby drugstore and asked if I wanted to come and work for her. They were short-staffed, and she could use my help. Since I didn't have anything else to do, I agreed.

On one of my first days working, I was straightening the shelves and everything on another shelf fell on me, knocking me to the floor. It didn't hurt, and I was fine, but I guess my brain used it as a way to release pent-up emotions because the next thing I knew, I was lying on the ground in a puddle of tears. The same manager who'd hired me told me to pull myself together and go home. When I called a couple of days later to find out my schedule, a co-worker said I wasn't on it. I left three different messages for the manager, and she never called me. I felt rejected again.

A few weeks later, I decided to look for another part-time job. I would need money after the baby was born. I felt so lost. Even though I was in therapy with Sally, had support from my host family, and a loving physician's support, I was flailing. I thought that maybe having a job would help me feel somewhat helpful. As it turned out, a person I met at college was the hiring manager for a local marketing firm. After we connected on the telephone, she invited me to come in for an interview. I hadn't told her I was pregnant. When I walked into her office, she stood and revealed a baby bump. We were both wearing the same maternity dress and we shared a laugh.

She hired me on the spot, and I started telemarketing for new services being rolled out by Bell South, our local telephone company. I sat in an open forum taking calls and helping mostly older people understand the difference between a rotary dial phone and a touch-tone phone. I loved helping them, and the money was decent.

One day after I left work, I was walking to the bus stop when I saw a woman I worked with at the shelter before my life turned crazy. I approached her, and she immediately recognized me. Surprised to see my baby bump, I explained everything to her while she patiently listened. When I was done explaining everything she asked if I would like to cover intake calls for battered women. My heart leaped with joy. I had really missed working with the shelter. We agreed to connect the next day and parted ways.

When I reached my bus stop, I realized that I missed my ride home by a few minutes. Even though it was spring it would be getting dark soon. With no money on me, I couldn't call home for a ride. All I had was a bus pass. I looked at the schedule posted inside the bus stop shelter, and no other buses were going to my part of town. I lived close enough to the subway station to walk, but I would have to wait for a bus to take me to the station nearby.

After waiting for almost an hour, a bus finally arrived and was going to the station that I needed. Arriving at the station, I caught the train headed for home, or so I'd thought. Once I settled into my seat, I was utterly exhausted and accidentally fell asleep. I woke to an older man shaking my shoulder.

"Miss, miss, miss," he seemed concerned.

When I finally came back to reality, the train had already stopped. It was pitch dark outside my window. I was covered in my drool, and I knew I had been asleep a lot longer than the fifteen minutes it was supposed to have taken for me to get to the Decatur station.

"Ma'am, I've been keeping you safe while you slept, especially since you're pregnant. Where is it that you're trying to go?" he asked with the kindest eyes.

"Where are we?" I was scared, and it showed.

"West End station, ma'am."

I jumped up, "Oh my god, oh my god, oh my god. How?"

"You fell asleep almost the minute we pulled out of Brookhaven. I didn't have the heart to wake you," his voice was like an angel.

The panic was erupting like a volcano, but he remained calm. The train doors closed, and we started heading east again. We were the only ones in that particular train car. My watch displayed the time. 9:30 p.m. I'd slept for nearly four hours! I thought about Lisa and Liam. They were probably losing their minds, not to mention I had broken every rule from curfew to failed check-ins.

"What do you need?" the stranger asked, genuinely concerned.

My hands instinctively covered my pregnant belly as the tears started flowing. I didn't know how to answer him. I wasn't asked that question often, although I had been asked it more in those last few months than most of my lifetime. He waited patiently while I searched inside for answers. "I need to get to the Decatur station and pray that buses are still running to my neighborhood. It's too late to walk."

The man asked how far I lived from the station, and when I told him it was only a few miles, he reached in his wallet and handed me cash for a taxi. As much as I resisted, he persisted, telling me that he had a daughter about my age and wouldn't want her stranded anywhere. I cried and thanked him a dozen times or more.

He rode the train with me to the other end of the line, close to an hour. He didn't say much, but his strong hand tightly held mine. I knew no harm would come to me. When we reached my final stop, I expected him to exit the train with me, but he stayed back. I hopped back on and gave him a long hug.

"Go, go," he urged. His smile lit up my world.

When I finally arrived safely home, no one was there. Inside, Lisa had taped a note to my bedroom door.

Allyson, we will be out pretty late tonight. Friends are in town, and we all gathered nearby. Here's their number if you need us! Sleep well! Xoxo

Relief washed over me that I hadn't worried them, but I felt like a complete failure. I couldn't shake the shame of my situation. No one understood the exhaustion that consumed my bones. I wasn't just physically tired; I was drained emotionally, spent spiritually, and defeated mentally. Years of narcissistic abuse were finally pounding on me, and it felt like too much.

I was pregnant with what I felt intuitively was a boy. He needed a solid foundation – something I had never been given. He needed nurturing, which I knew I was more than capable of giving him, and that's what hurt so much. What I lacked in every other area of my life, I thrived in the giving love department. I already loved him. That part was easy.

I contacted Sister Mary the next day and told her I was ready to select my baby's adoptive parents from the profiles she had on file. Little did I know that as lost as I felt, the process of choosing who would parent my son would lead me down a path that would forever alter my life.

Decisions

Have you ever made a decision that couldn't be changed once you made it?

Yes _____ No_____ I'm not sure _____

If you're not sure, these life changes could include:

- Getting married
- Getting divorced
- Getting pregnant
- Making a major move
- Quitting a job
- Accepting a promotion
- Committing to being a caregiver

While it's true that any of the above can be reversed, very few of us quickly reverse big decisions. Mostly because we are afraid of what other people will think. Studies reveal that most people would rather live with regret than disappoint people. Take a moment and allow that to sink in.

Our society has attached shame and guilt to:

- Divorce
- Leaving the altar mid-vow
- Abortion and Adoption
- Leaving a job we just started
- Moving back home after a huge move

Most people choose to see the above list as failures. Maybe you do, as well.

Sit with your major decisions today. Are you happy? If not, are you willing to do whatever it takes to embrace happiness? Is that going to require that you "undo" something you've done? If so, what does that look like?

Be honest. Be brave enough to tell yourself the truth. You deserve your heart's desires.

CHAPTER EIGHT

LOVING ARMS

When I entered the woman's office, her hair was flaming red, the shade that only comes from a bottle, with lipstick to match. Her fingers donned long, fake red nails. Even her shoes were red. Her presentation was bold, if not a little harsh, but underneath was a beautifully kind and caring woman. She introduced herself as Rebecca, the "sad day" lady. Her job was to present prospective parents to birthmothers so that they would feel some control in the adoption process.

We sat down at a round table covered in files. There were dozens of hopeful parents that had submitted letters to Catholic Services. In 1985, Georgia was a closed-adoption state, meaning that we couldn't pass any identifying information between us, including photographs. Even the letters from hopeful parents were only signed with their initials.

Rebecca gave me the official instruction on selecting the parents for my son. She offered to look at their backstory and choose from the common interests we shared. That didn't feel right to me, and she immediately sensed my hesitation.

"Come with me," Rebecca stood and walked toward a tiny room at the end of the hallway.

I obediently followed her, and she showed me a nook I hadn't seen before. It was dark with pillows on the floor.

"This is our meditation slash prayer room. I will show you a technique I think will help you figure this out. Are you open?"

I didn't answer. Instead, I found my way to a pillow and carefully plopped my very pregnant body down. Rebecca took her place across from me. Then, she guided me through imagining my baby in the arms of his parents. I interrupted her by sharing Napoleon Hill's book *Think and Grow Rich* and how I used his philosophies to help me when I lived in my car. She was fascinated by my journey of being rescued and seeing the tiny flowers on the curtains.

"That's *exactly* what I'm talking about!" she exclaimed. "Use this same method, and you'll know who to choose."

Rebecca left me to meditate. At first, it was difficult. I didn't want to see my baby in the arms of anyone else. I wanted him with me! But, deep down, I knew I was ill-equipped to handle such a huge responsibility. So, I would go to that room often and meditate.

I pictured my son's parents as very stable. They didn't have to be wealthy or connected. I just wanted them to have their shit together emotionally more than anything. I also wanted his mother, especially, to understand my plight and the sacrifice I was making, not for any type of reward, but in hopes that it would somehow make her appreciate my son – our son – even more.

As I meditated, I imagined his mother holding him on my shoulder. I would sit in the dimly lit room and rock an imaginary bundle back and forth. I would often swear that I could feel his skin against my cheek and smell him. My heart would fill with joy and gratitude for parenting him and being explicitly chosen to love the bundle of joy.

After meditating, I would find Rebecca, and we would sit at the table. She would hand me stacks of letters to read, and after only a few sentences, I would nod my head and place them in the rejection pile. She was losing her patience with me, and she and the nuns would whisper about me. I couldn't always make out exactly what they were saying, but the little bit I did pick up on, I knew they were making assumptions that I wasn't serious about the process or that I was being too picky or irresponsible. Rebecca also resorted to passive-aggressive remarks about how other girls in the program chose quickly.

"Good for them," I would always retort.

No matter how many letters I read, I just couldn't make a decision. Even though I was annoying myself, I refused to pick just anyone. I was nearing the end of my pregnancy, and Sister Mary called me to schedule my last appointment with her. We both knew what this meant. I needed to choose a family. The night before visiting her office I didn't sleep. Instead, I kept thinking about this woman who was at home waiting to be a mother. She must have experienced fear daily, hoping and praying that someone would choose her to parent their child. Still, though, none of the letters I read felt right.

The next day I sat with Sister Mary. We had already shared some pretty contentious conversations. For instance, she wanted me to sign the adoption papers before my son was born. I refused. She wanted my son whisked away from me right after he was born and for me to never see him again. I refused. She wanted me to spend only a few minutes with him as a compromise, but I declined. So, I was not her favorite unwed mother. Regardless, I held a precious commodity in my belly, and we both knew it. I used it to my full advantage. This adoption was going my way or no way at all.

Sister Mary handed me a stack of letters. "Read these, please, all the way through to the end, if you don't mind. It might help you choose a better act. Read the letters, Allyson." She was displeased.

"No, thank you," I stared her down.

"What is your problem? If you want to keep the child, then just let us know, but otherwise, we have our processes, Allyson." Her habit couldn't hide her frustration.

"I don't really give a damn about your processes, excuse my French. This is my son we are talking about, and I'm not just going to choose a couple simply because they have a nursery ready, attend church, and are infertile!" I was positive the entire floor had heard me. I was heated.

Sister Mary stood and went to find Rebecca; I was sure of it. Meanwhile, I looked out the window, and down below on the sidewalk stood a fellow birth mother who had given birth already. Her belly was still full, and now she just looked swollen and sad. With no baby to hold, no one would forgive her plump body. Our society is so cruel about that. I looked down at my thighs and thought about the hundred or more extra pounds I was carrying. I swallowed a lump growing in my throat. My body would never be the same, and yet, I would have nothing to show for it. I thought about Billy rubbing my tummy during the short stint that he was excited and we were good. I had made some comment about becoming a whale, and he was quick to tell me that whales were his favorite sea creature. I was snapped back to reality by Rebecca. She was leaning against the door jamb and irritated. Before she could speak a word, I gave my three-minute speech about *my* process.

"If you can't decide, we will just decide for you," Rebecca was haughty.

"Then I won't place him. I'll figure it out. I always do." I stood and gathered my belongings. I was waiting for the doors to open at the elevator when Sister Mary found me.

"Allyson, what's on your wish list?" Her eyes were pleading.

"Like you give a shit. It's been three months of me coming here every week, sitting in your shitty dark room, reading your pathetic letters, and *now* you ask?" I was so pissed, and now I had an attentive audience. "To make matters worse, you're all acting like I'm at the fucking grocery store picking out cereal! I *love my baby!* Did that ever occur to any of you?" Sister Mary sat down in the lobby area and asked me to join her, but I refused.

The elevator doors opened, but before I could step in, Sister Mary practically begged me to stay, "Allyson, *please! Please!* You've been through so much, and you're still going through so much. Perhaps we've let you down in this process."

Before she could finish, I had to have my final say, "Perhaps? You're kidding, right?! I mean, I do appreciate everything you've done for me. You gave me shelter and food. That's very nice of you, but the only reason is that I have something you desperately want, and that is sort of sick to me. Now, this bullshit! You won't back me into a corner, Sister Mary! That won't happen; I don't care what you've done for me. None of it has been out of the kindness of anyone's heart! You're just here doing your job, and Rebecca played nicely in the beginning, but now that I won't just give a head nod to any pair of shit parents, I'm suddenly the problem. I would tell you to fuck yourself, but I'm trying to respect that you love Jesus and work for him in some capacity, but if you didn't, that's what I would be saying to you! You crossed the line with me today!" I was spiraling and my words echoed off the walls.

Instead of allowing her to react, I found the staircase and made my way outside. It just so happened that my bus was pulling up at that very moment, and I climbed on it. When I glanced back, Rebecca was on the sidewalk. She'd made a mad dash for me. I was pissed! Ten minutes into the bus ride, I wondered if my belongings would be by the curb when I arrived home. After all, if I didn't follow their rules, I was out of the program, which meant no more housing for me. Now, I also had no car and wasn't sure where I would land. None of that mattered, though, because I was done being manipulated.

When I arrived home Lisa was standing in the driveway waiting for me. She invited me to take a walk with her, so I quickly put my things away, changed shoes, and joined her outside. I loved walking in the neighborhood, especially with her. We would talk about her family, the kids, recipes, but I knew today's talk would be different. It was apparent she'd received a call about me and the situation.

As we walked, Lisa confirmed that Sister Mary had called, but then she surprised me. Sister Mary confessed that she had let me down and that any anger I was experiencing would be natural for anyone in my situation. It didn't feel like manipulation coming from Lisa. I trusted her implicitly. Instead, from Lisa's perspective, it seemed that most other unwed mothers were teenagers and just did what they were told.

They hadn't considered that I was an adult and probably needed to be treated as such.

I confessed to Lisa that I had gone off on Sister Mary and felt guilty for it but only because she was a nun. Lisa chuckled and then told me how she'd gone off on a priest who wouldn't listen to her point of view during a church fundraising meeting. It made me feel like less of a problem. Then, Lisa told me that Sister Mary would like the chance to make things right with me and implored Lisa to bring me back the following day. I reluctantly agreed and told Lisa that if things were anything like they turned out that day, I would leave immediately. She agreed.

The following day, Lisa and I met with Sister Mary once again. When we arrived, Lisa wanted to stay in her car and assured me that she would be right there if I wanted to leave. She even promised to leave the car running if that would make me feel better. We shared a laugh like we always did.

When I entered the building, I was surprised to see Sister Mary waiting for me on the bottom floor. She thanked me for seeing her and motioned me to a small office adjacent to the lobby. I joked that no one wanted to see me upstairs, but she didn't laugh or even crack a smile.

"What do you want, Allyson?" It was gentle and sincere.

"I want to choose parents that feel right." It was the calmest I ever felt with her.

"What's your wishlist?" She was being serious.

"If you're serious, I would love to share it with you." I sat back in my chair, and Braxton Hicks contractions started. I'd had them for days.

"Go on," Sister Mary removed a notepad and pen from a pocket under her habit.

I gave her my list. It was simple—new parents. No children. Animal lovers. A solid marriage. A couple who would understand my pain. Sister Mary stopped and looked deep into my eyes.

"Has that been the issue all along? That no one in the letters you've read seems to understand what you're going through?"

I nodded and felt hot tears forming. I was ready to hear a speech about how impossible I was being and that no one could ever understand my pain. Instead, something completely different happened.

Sister Mary stood. "Don't move. I'll be right back."

She left me in the small room, and I felt utterly alone for the first time in a while. I don't know what it was about the space that made me feel sad, but I wouldn't say I liked it. I contemplated leaving, but Sister Mary returned quickly. She took her seat and handed me a yellow envelope. It was addressed to Catholic Services. Someone had already opened it because it was torn at the top. The return address was inked out. I retrieved the contents, a two-page letter, and began reading.

Dear fellow birthmother,

I've been where you are right now. When I was a teenager, I placed a son for adoption. Now, I find myself unable to carry a baby to full term for whatever reason. I have been pregnant several times, and now my doctor is telling me (and my husband) that another viable pregnancy isn't possible.

Holding the letter to my chest, I rocked back and forth. This was the woman I had felt early on in this process. Her heart was the one connecting with me during my meditations. I felt the tears roll down my face. There were many more words on the pages, but they weren't necessary. My decision was made. "This is it," I handed the letter to Sister Mary.

I stood up and turned to leave when I felt her hand on my shoulder. When I turned to face Sister Mary, tears ran down her face. "Even as a sister in Christ, Allyson, I make mistakes. None of us are perfect." She finally looked real to me.

Before I could say anything, she reached for me, and I hugged her. We had never before embraced, and it was long overdue. We were both crying, and there was so much in our tears. It felt like we were apologizing, agreeing, understanding, seeing, and feeling the presence of God all wrapped into one tight embrace. It lasted several minutes.

Finally, we broke away from one another. Without saying a word, we left that small room, and I knew there was nothing left for us to do. The preparation was all done. Now, the only thing we were all waiting for was the birth of our son.

The Danger of Spiritual Bypassing

Did you know that you can be spiritual and cuss?

Did you know that it's normal and natural to feel extreme anger and still be spiritual?

Years after placing my son, I ran into Sister Mary at a fundraiser for battered women. She reveled in how calm I seemed. I lovingly reminded her that I had every reason to be angry. She didn't disagree. In fact, we had an open conversation about the dangers of repressing our anger.

Are you angry?
Yes! _____
Not right now, but give me a minute and I could be _____
No, I've worked through it _____

If you are easily triggered, you're angry. What triggers you?

- The past
- Behavior I disagree with
- The future
- A particular person
- A smell, food, or other things
- A place

In order for the trigger to stop, what needs to heal inside of you?

_____

_____

_____

_____

_____

_____

What are you most afraid of happening if you do the work to heal yourself?

_____

_____

_____

_____

_____

If you did the work to heal yourself, what is the best possible outcome you can imagine?

_____

_____

_____

_____

Remember this. You are human. It's perfectly natural for you to FEEL your feelings even if those are anger, sadness and fear. In reality, it's the only way you can authentically heal.

CHAPTER NINE

IT'S A BOY

It was thirty-six long hours of back labor. Dr. Moussakhani wouldn't perform a C-section because he said that the scar on my heart was going to be tough enough and he didn't want one on my body, too. My son stayed calm throughout the entire labor so they let him come into the world on his terms.

As soon as he was born, the delivery room became somewhat chaotic. At first, I thought it was because they were taking him away from me, but after that emotional encounter with Sister Mary, we now had a special relationship. What I didn't know, what none of us knew, was that my son had severe ligamentous laxity. In other words, his feet were facing backward. This would mean extensive treatment for him, which would include multiple surgeries. The news was a huge blow and I again felt like I had failed somehow.

One of the heavy burdens weighing on me was how I was going to be able to walk away from him knowing that he needed me more than ever. He seemed so helpless and each time I held him, which was a lot, he stared so deeply into my eyes. It was tough to hold him and impossible to put him down. Because I had been so strong about being treated as his mother, with all the same privileges in the hospital, he was rooming in with me. The feeling of finally having him in my arms was amazing.

Every moment the staff was amazing. Dr. Moussakhani was with me every step of the way. He visited me the morning after my son was born, and made sure to see me at least once, if not twice, each day while I was in the hospital. He was so careful with choosing his words, and at one point he thought I'd changed my mind about the adoption. What I didn't share with anyone was that I was plagued with second thoughts.

The hospital couldn't release me because I woke every day with a slight fever. One day turned into two and two days into three. I took it as a gift from the Universe and milked every second with my son.

On the third day of our stay, my mother showed up in my room. She was raving about how gorgeous my baby was and commented on how much weight I had gained. Each time a nurse came in the room, which was a lot because of my son's legs, she would tell them how I was keeping her grandson from living with her or knowing her. Of course, the entire staff knew my history and no one paid any attention to her. She also tried to gaslight me by saying that I had blown everything out of proportion and how she stayed up nights worrying about me. Yet, she never called the police or put out any sort of missing persons report on me. I had already checked, out of curiosity.

Finally, when the staff had had enough, they asked her to please leave the hospital. But, of course, she was back the morning that I signed the adoption papers because no one else wanted to come and get me. No one else wanted to deal with my emotions. My family, even though they had never been there for me before, all wanted my son. Not me – just him. It was a huge slap in my face.

The night before I left the hospital, though, I was struggling. I had no idea what to do about my son, myself, or life in general. Some of the nurses gave me pamphlets about Section 8 housing, food stamps, and other assistance while other nurses were more encouraging about adoption. My doctor and the pediatrician remained pretty neutral, as did Sister Mary to my surprise. She visited several times and never swayed me one way or the other.

Sally, my therapist, was on speed dial. She had a pager and gave me her home telephone number. Oddly enough, I didn't call her or anyone. I found myself in a cocoon in my room. But my last night at the hospital was different. I finally called her. When she picked up, I couldn't speak.

"Allyson, is this you? Hello?" she sounded frantic.

"It's me," I managed to whisper.

"How…how are you?" Sally sounded worried.

"I'm scared." It was the most honest I had been with myself.

"I'm on my way," Sally said then hung up. I knew she didn't want to hear me protesting her plan.

A little later Sally showed up. My son was sound asleep next to me in a bassinet. She hadn't seen him, so she took time to softly squeal, sharing how beautiful she thought he was, and that he looked just like me, which he did. After she settled in, we got serious about my adoption plan.

Hours passed, it was late, and Sally needed to leave. I called the nursery and had my son taken down the hall so I could think. It was just past midnight when I was finally alone in my room. The lights were off with only a street light shining through my window. It occurred to me as I paced the floor that it was my one-year anniversary with Billy. My heart sank. There'd been so much loss in just a twelve-month period. It was hard to wrap my brain around it all.

Even though placing my son for adoption made the most logical sense, I couldn't seem to bring myself to do it. My fever was definitely gone, and I knew I would be discharged in eight hours, which meant I would either have to sign the adoption papers or leave the hospital with my son. The time to wait was over.

I fell to the floor weeping. The agony overwhelmed every part of me. I didn't know what to do. I always knew what to do, and if I didn't, my intuition was a great guide. But every time I went to listen for guidance, it was empty. Silence filled me. I was so angry at God. *Why now?!* Every other time I needed to take the next step on this journey, I heard exactly what to do. Here I was, with hours pressing down on me, and I was met with abandonment. I didn't understand.

Sitting in a corner with my back pressed against the wall, I wrapped myself in a blanket from the bed. Even though it was summer, I was shivering from head to toe while simultaneously sweating. Nothing made sense. I felt as though I was going insane.

A nurse came into my room. She was large and in charge. Her mocha skin was shiny and she smelled of coconut. She had a pink flower tucked behind her ear, which I thought odd of a nurse, but I didn't say anything about it. She sat on the bed facing me and motioned for me to come and sit next to her. Without either of us saying a word, I stood and joined her.

"How are you, child?" she asked sweetly.

For the first time since I had been there, I had nothing to say. I sat staring at the floor thinking that I was missing time with my son. It also hit me that I wouldn't be with him the next night if I decided to go through with my original plan.

"You know, oftentimes the best decision isn't the easy one," the nurse's voice was soft but solid. She reached for my hand and I allowed her to hold it. Her hand was soft as velvet. She continued, "You may feel punished right now, but later in life this time is going to make sense. You'll look back and understand why you made every decision to get you to this point."

I interrupted her, "Do I know you?" Because it certainly seemed as though she knew me.

She smiled and didn't answer but continued, "You're struggling now, but you know what to do. Just follow your heart. You'll see."

The nurse released my hand, stood and left. I never saw her again.

The numbness took over me. I sat staring at the white floor. The light from the bathroom illuminated the room. My arm hurt from the I.V. and it throbbed, but everything else was numb, especially my brain. I kept closing my eyes and every time I did, all I could see were my son's blue eyes staring back at me.

Before I realized it, I was on my knees on the floor, pulling my hair, and crying out to God.

"Why have you betrayed me when I need you the most?" I heard myself almost barking. I didn't recognize my own voice. It was filled with desperation. "Talk to me! Damn it!"

I cried even harder. "I don't know what to do!"

Then, just like that, I heard the voice I hadn't heard in months. It was that same male voice in my mind. *You do know. You've already been shown.*

"I can't do it," I wailed on the floor. "I'm sorry! I can't do this! I can't! It's too hard! I can't live without him. I'll die. I just know it! I'm sorry, God! I'm so sorry!" I cried so hard I thought my eyeballs would pop out from their sockets.

After a little while, I calmed down enough to pick myself up from the floor and walk to my bathroom sink. Looking in the mirror, I saw a stranger staring back at me. She was swollen, overweight, bleeding profusely, with sore breasts that had to be stopped from producing her baby's milk, and ratted hair that desperately needed shampooing. I was a wreck. I had bitten my fingernails down to the quicks and they were bloody and sore. I had picked my toenails off and my skin was raw on my feet. I looked and felt like a mental ward patient.

I pressed the call button for the nurse. A blonde woman appeared quickly. I told her that I wanted to see the black nurse with a pink flower resting behind her ear. The nurse had no idea who I was referring to. I persisted and explained that she had just been in my room. The nurse shrugged, still clueless.

"May I help you, dear? You called for a nurse," she was pushy.

I told her that I wanted to shower and clean up. She looked at hands and feet, and suggested some ointment, too. She showed me to a bathroom down the hallway, and I stood under the shower for what felt like an eternity. Washing my hair, shaving my body, and cleaning blood off helped restore me to balance. I also smelled good again, and that helped. It wasn't like me to not groom. Maybe my crisis was bigger than even I understood.

Back in my room, I dried my hair, brushed and flossed my teeth, and climbed into bed. It was 2 a.m. Time was slipping away. I knew that sleep was impossible, so I got back out of bed and walked to the nursery. Through the glass window lay my son. He was sound asleep right in the front row. I pressed my cheek against the glass and stared at him for what felt like hours.

When I felt that I couldn't stand another second, I returned to my room. My insides felt like a caged tiger. I remember my grandmother always saying that there was no rest for the weary. I never understood it until that moment. My soul was at unrest and I was standing at a major crossroads.

Once again, I found myself on my knees, but this time much calmer. I rocked back and forth as I had done so many times when I was trying to manifest my son's adoptive parents. I thought rocking might help bring that feeling back, which would provide some clarity for me.

Out of nowhere I heard, "Allyson." It was commanding and continued, "If you sign the adoption papers, you'll see him again."

"No, I won't," I heard myself say aloud. "Georgia is a closed state. It'll be impossible to find him"

Twice more I heard, "If you sign the papers, you'll see him again."

The next morning, Sister Mary arrived with a woman I had never met before. She had a stack of papers in her hands with a notary seal. There were no introductions. We sat at a small table in my room and she handed me paper after paper explaining that I was surrendering all of my rights to my son. I signed my name to all of them, and as soon as it was finished, a nurse put a needle in my arm and medicated me.

Even with the medicine, I screamed as I watched my little boy be wheeled away from my room. I ran after him, but one of the nurses grabbed me and held me close to her. I fell to the floor in anguish. I could hear several nurses sniffling as they fought back tears. It was the worst day of my life.

Difficult Things I've Learned

The best decision isn't always the easiest. The danger in this is that it's easy to get stuck in a victim mentality when we make decisions that break our hearts.

What's the most painful decision you've ever made?

Are you willing to take full responsibility for making the decision? In other words, are you willing to release any blame you feel toward others and own your choices?

Yes! _____ Not yet, but I'm getting there _____

Once you own your choices, you have your power back. That's right! Owning your decisions is the first step in reclaiming your life! From that place, you can finally start to make healthier steps on your life path.

What's a step I know I need to take right now in order to guide my life in a better direction?

On a scale of 1-10, with one being a "nope, not really" and 10 being a big "hell, yes," how willing am I to take a chance on myself?
1 2 3 4 5 6 7 8 9 10 (circle one)

Now, looking at the number you chose, what's keeping you from choosing "10?"

_____

_____

_____

_____

_____

If you chose "10," what steps will you be taking today?

_____

_____

_____

_____

Congratulations for taking this first inspired action to begin moving and showing up in a completely different way. Only you can stop regretting it. Only you can come into full acceptance of the choices you've made. Only you can do the self-forgiveness that is needed. Only you can make a new choice.

CHAPTER TEN

TWENTY-FOUR YEARS LATER

Allyson, wake up! Wake up! Wake up! It's time! It was the voice – my guide's voice. I sat straight up in bed. It was exactly 3:33 a.m. There was no hesitation. I knew exactly what was happening.

My daughter was sound asleep in her bed, and even though I knew she would want to hear this news, it was a school night. I never kept her from knowing about her half-brother and reminded her every year on his birthday about the message I received so many years before in my hospital room.

Sitting in the kitchen sipping coffee, I grabbed my laptop and googled Catholic Social Services. My stomach flipped. The office opened at 8 a.m. and they had a special department, still after all the years, specifically for adoption.

I sat outside as soon as the sky lightened and watched the sunrise over the trees. It was a new day. The feeling in my stomach was joy, and I knew the day held something special.

At exactly 8 a.m. I called the number listed on the website. I made my way through the receptionist and to a woman who introduced herself as a social worker. After explaining who I was and why I was calling, she immediately turned my hopes upside down. I was discouraged from the very beginning of the search for my son. The social worker told me it would be expensive and take years. After an in-depth conversation, she finally realized that I wasn't giving up and agreed to send the paperwork by fax to start the process.

Completing those papers was my only priority that day, but I also had to see Laura off to school. So, I walked her outside, closed her car door, gave her a kiss on the cheek, and kept the news to myself just in case nothing came of it. After all, I had just been told that in order for Catholic Services to reunite us, my son would also have to send in papers to find me. Since he was only twenty-four, I wasn't sure that would happen. But there was the voice that morning.

I poured my third or fourth cup of coffee and sat down to complete a stack of papers. It took some time, but feeling confident that I answered everything thoroughly, I faxed the papers back. Catholic Services needed money from me, too, so I filled out the check, placed it in an envelope, and rushed it to the post office for a faster delivery downtown.

The day went on as usual. That afternoon Laura returned home from school, changed her clothes and left again for her job at a local ice cream place. I grocery shopped and prepared dinner for us. When she finally returned home, we ate and that's when I shared with her everything that had happened earlier in the day. She was cautiously optimistic and being one of my staunch protectors, she asked me to stay grounded and not get my hopes up too high. I agreed.

Late in the morning the next day, my landline rang. It was rare to have anyone call that number, and I assumed it was a sales call until I looked at the caller I.D. "Catholic Services" was displayed clearly on the screen.

I snatched up the phone, "Hello!"

"Hi, is this Allyson?" the woman asked.

"It is." I felt my blood rushing through my veins.

"Are you sitting down?" she continued with her questions.

"Oh, God! What's wrong?" My heart immediately sank.

Before I could get any more upset, she quickly reassured me that everything was fine. It took me a moment to believe her, but she was finally convincing enough that I settled down.

"So, what's going on? Why are you calling me so soon after faxing my paperwork to you yesterday?" It was as if I was right back in that building defending myself and my son all over again.

"Well, I don't think this has ever happened before," her voice was shaking. "You see, we received two faxes this morning, and after going over them both, we realized that we were looking at yours and your son's paperwork. You each faxed your papers just minutes apart from each other." She was emotional.

If you sign the papers, you'll see him again. That voice rang through my head. I fell into my chair. The social worker could hear me crying and we had a moment together.

After I composed myself, I asked when I could see him, and she promised to arrange it right away, which she did. Just five days later, in the very same room where I spent many counseling sessions, we embraced for the very first time. I learned that he suffered from lung issues, surgeries for his feet, and depression for most of his life. He assured me it wasn't because he was adopted. To this day, I have my doubts.

A few months later, I attended his wedding alongside his parents. It was a miracle to be present for it. After that, we had a handful of visits, and I feel that maybe it was too complicated for us both, so those visits faded away.

My heart is full, however, because God's promise was that I would see my son again, and I did. I'd made the gut-wrenching decision to place him for adoption, and along with that decision came the understanding that I'm not his mom. I am his birth mother and am very proud to hold that role so dear to my heart. I, however, am not his mom. I accept that.

Life isn't always easy, and I don't believe that we are here for the easy road, though some of us stay on an imaginary one thinking that avoiding pain is the answer to peace. It isn't.

What this journey taught me is that we came into this world with a connection to the other side. That connection is present as a gift for our sanity. Listening and following our gut instincts is not always the easier path. In fact, at times it can be the absolute hardest choice at the moment. However, the rewards that come with it far outweigh immediate gratification.

My son was given life. He married an amazing woman with a beautiful soul. Together, they've built a joyful, compassionate, and eternal bond that most people only hope to experience. I gave them that chance to find one another and share their amazing love. That was my mission.

We have more than one mission. Don't ever forget it.

The thing you must always remember and grow to understand is that your life has deeper meaning than you can comprehend. Your path to finding it is to heal yourself daily, tap into your soul, listen and follow the guidance you receive. If you follow this recipe for life, you will have peace that surpasses all understanding and your life will make more and more sense as you go.

Thank you for allowing me to share this journey. I hope it inspires you to be everything and experience all that your heart desires. I see you. I hear you. I love you. Namaste!

The Promise

What promise are you willing to make to yourself that will motivate you to stay on a healing path?

If you should start to slip back into old patterns of behavior, who has your back that will help you get back on track again? What plan will you put in place with them?

My hope for you is that you come to realize that transformation takes commitment and the understanding that you must look at your pain in order to find your power.

ABOUT ALLYSON

Allyson Roberts knows what it takes to make it in this world. As a young woman who found herself homeless, pregnant, and forced to live in her car, she turned to the writing of Napoleon Hill for comfort and guidance. Little did she know then what a huge impact his philosophies would make on her life. As a cognitive-behavioral expert along with her natural intuition, Allyson has guided thousands of people all over the world to find their internal power.

From intimate one-on-one conversations to speaking at live events, Allyson uses her training to overcome trauma, childhood issues, self-worth struggles, and more. In her sessions, she utilizes her professional training, as well as her natural gifts and strategic life coaching experience to bring people from all walks of life to their unique purpose.

Allyson is the founder of Outrageous Freedom now known as Unapologetic Power, LLC, and best-selling programs such as *Stop Shilting on Yourself, Painless Pivots to Power, and Unapologetic Power.* Her book, *The Magic in You*, is available in her blog series.

A Special Gift from Allyson

Now that you've read *The Spiritual Journey: The Part No One Talks About*, you are on your way to understanding that even when the world seems to be falling apart, you are a powerful manifestor! Plus … I hope my story has helped you understand how much you are loved by the Universe and that perfection is not expected of you in order to build the life you want to live.

You'll also receive the special bonus I created to add to your toolkit … **The Reset**, which is a guided meditation for you to connect with your angels, guides, and masters so that you can wipe your emotional slate clean and continue your journey feeling renewed.

There's so much confusing information out there about spirituality and manifesting. Having finished reading this book, you are now armed with what you need to know about creating the life your heart desires without having to do it perfectly or be perfect.

While this meditation is offered for sale, just go to the link below and tell us where to send it.

https://www.allysonroberts.com/resetmeditation

The sooner you know how to begin visualizing and attracting everything you want into your life, the better your chances of no longer attracting the things you *don't want!*

I'm in your corner. Let me know if I can help further.

Here's to manifesting your best life!

Best,